· REVISED & ENLARGED ·

HERE'S THE
DIFFERENCE

BRINGING IMPORTANT
BIBLICAL DISTINCTIONS
INTO FOCUS

Some books by William MacDonald

Armageddon Soon?
Believer's Bible Commentary
Christ Loved the Church
God's Answers to Man's Questions
Grasping for Shadows
Lord, Break Me
My Heart, My Life, My All
Once in Christ, In Christ Forever
One Day at a Time
True Discipleship
The Forgotten Command: Be Holy
The Wonders of God
Worlds Apart

• REVISED & ENLARGED •

HERE'S THE
DIFFERENCE

BRINGING IMPORTANT
BIBLICAL DISTINCTIONS
INTO FOCUS

William MacDonald

GOSPEL FOLIO PRESS
304 Killaly St. West Port Colborne, ON L3K 6A6
Available in the UK from JOHN RITCHIE LTD.
40 Beansburn, Kilmarnock, Scotland

This edition is a major revision of a previous book by the same title, published by Walterick Publishers.

Published by Gospel Folio Press
304 Killaly St. West Port Colborne, ON L3K 6A6

Unless otherwise indicated, Scripture references are from the New King James Version, copyright © 1979, 1980, 1982, 1985 by Thomas Nelson, Inc., Nashville, Tennessee. Used by permission.

Abbreviations

ASV   American Standard Version
KJV   King James Version
NASB New American Standard Bible
NKJV New King James Version
NIV   New International Version
RSV   Revised Standard Version

ISBN 1-882701-45-3

Cover design by J. B. Nicholson, Jr.

Printed in the United States of America

Contents

Part IV: DISTINCTIONS IN FUTURE EVENTS

Part V: OTHER DISTINCTIONS IN SCRIPTURE

Foreword

The purpose of this book is to provide some valuable keys for studying the Scriptures, especially the New Testament. Every believer *should* be a Bible student. Every believer *can* be a Bible student. But most of us need help in how to do it. The chapters that follow are designed to provide some help.

The reader will learn that definitions are important. Biblical words have meanings that are not found in the regular dictionary. A "mystery" in the Word of God is not the same as it is in common usage.

Doctrinal accuracy is important. All scriptures dealing with a subject must be considered in order to reach a proper understanding.

It is important to distinguish things that differ. There are passages in one Gospel that *seem* to be the same as found in another Gospel. However, when studied in their context, it is clear that they teach completely different lessons.

Many subjects—like justification and sanctification—have different phases; and some events—like the coming of the Lord—have different stages. To see this often avoids considerable confusion.

Believers who studied the earlier edition of *Here's the Difference* uniformly agreed that it was a distinct help in opening the Word to them and increasing the thrill of Bible study. Now as it is sent forth in an enlarged edition, our hope is that the benefits will be multiplied.

—THE PUBLISHERS

Part I
DISTINCTIONS IN SALVATION

1
Three Tenses of Salvation

When we first become Christians, most of us can think of only one type of salvation, the salvation of our *souls*. In our Bible study we automatically try to fit this meaning into every occurrence of the word. But sooner or later we will find out that it won't always fit.

Then we come to realize that *salvation* is a very general word meaning "deliverance," "safety," or "soundness." In Philippians 1:19, for example, Paul uses it concerning his expected release from prison:

> *For I know that this shall turn to my **salvation** through your prayer and the supply of the Spirit of Jesus Christ* (KJV). (The New King James Version helpfully translates the word "deliverance" in this context.)

In Philippians 2:12, *salvation* means something quite different; it means the solution of a problem that had broken out in the church at Philippi. A serious case of disunity had arisen (Phil. 2:14; 4:2). Paul reminds the Christians that the answer to the problem was for them all to have the humble, self-sacrificing mind of the Lord Jesus. Then in 2:12 he says:

> *Therefore, my beloved, as you have always obeyed, not as in my presence only, but now much more in my absence, **work out your own salvation** with fear and trembling.*

11

In other words, "I have told you the way of deliverance from the problem that vexes you. Now work out the solution with fear and trembling."

In three passages *salvation* is used to describe deliverance from drowning:

> 30 *And as the sailors were seeking to escape from the ship, when they had let down the skiff into the sea, under pretense of putting out anchors from the prow,* 31 *Paul said to the centurion and to the soldiers, "Unless these men stay in the ship, you cannot **be saved** "* (Acts 27:30-31).

> *By faith Noah, being divinely warned of things not yet seen, moved with godly fear, prepared an ark for the **saving** of his household...* (Heb. 11:7a).

> 19 *...He went and preached to the spirits in prison,* 20 *who formerly were disobedient, when once the Divine longsuffering waited in the days of Noah, while the ark was being prepared, in which a few, that is, eight souls, were **saved** through water* (1 Pet. 3:19-20).

God is the Savior of all men in the sense that He preserves and sustains them:

> *For to this end we both labor and suffer reproach, because we trust in the living God, who is the **Savior** of all men, especially of those who believe* (1 Tim. 4:10).

But the uses of the words *salvation* or *saved* in which we are principally interested are those which have to do with deliverance from sin. This is a very common meaning in the New Testament.

Here we must learn to distinguish the three tenses of salvation—past, present, and future:

Past—I was saved from the penalty of sin: justification.

Present—I am being saved from the power of sin: sanctification.

Future—I shall be saved from the presence of sin: glorification.

Past Tense

Here are some verses which speak primarily of salvation from the penalty of sin:

*For by grace **you have been saved** through faith, and that not of yourselves; it is the gift of God* (Eph. 2:8).

*[God] who **has saved** us and called us with a holy calling...* (2 Tim. 1:9a).

*Not by works of righteousness which we have done, but according to His mercy **He saved** us, through the washing of regeneration and renewing of the Holy Spirit* (Titus 3:5).

Notice that in these three examples the word *saved* is in the past tense. However, there are other verses which speak of our deliverance from the penalty of sin where the verb is *not* in the past tense.

*Nor is there **salvation** in any other, for there is no other name under heaven given among men by which **we must be saved*** (Acts 4:12).

*That if you confess with your mouth the Lord Jesus and believe in your heart that God has raised Him from the dead, **you will be saved*** (Rom. 10:9).

So you must decide by the *contents* of the verse rather than by the *tense* of the verb whether the past tense of salvation is meant. If the subject is the once-for-all deliverance from the condemnation of sin, then you know it refers to the past tense of salvation.

Present Tense

Although it's true that I *have been* saved, it is equally true that I am *being* saved day by day. I have been saved from damnation; I am being saved from damage. I have been saved from the penalty of sin; I am being saved from the power of sin. I have been saved through the finished work of Christ on the Cross; I am being saved through His life and ministry for me at the right hand of God. That is what is meant, for example, in Romans 5:10:

*For if when we were enemies we were reconciled to God through the death of His Son, much more, having been reconciled, **we shall be saved** by His life.*

The present tense of salvation is much the same as sanctification—the process of being separated to God from sin and defilement. It is this salvation as a continuing process that we read about in Hebrews 7:25:

*Therefore He is also able **to save** to the uttermost those who come to God through Him, since He always lives to make intercession for them.*

Still another passage where we find the present tense is 1 Corinthians 1:18:

*For the message of the cross is foolishness to those who are perishing, but to us who **are being saved** it is the power of God.*

14

Future Tense

Finally, there is the future aspect of salvation. When we meet the Savior face-to-face, we *shall be* saved from sin's presence. Our bodies will be redeemed and glorified. The following verses describe the glorious future consummation of our salvation:

*...For now our **salvation** is nearer than when we first believed* (Rom. 13:11b).

8 *But let us who are of the day be sober, putting on the breastplate of faith and love, and as a helmet **the hope of salvation**.* 9 *For God did not appoint us to wrath, but **to obtain salvation** through our Lord Jesus Christ* (1 Thess. 5:8-9).

...To those who eagerly wait for Him He will appear a second time, apart from sin, for salvation (Heb. 9:28b).

[You] *who are kept by the power of God through faith **for salvation** ready to be revealed in the last time* (1 Pet. 1:5).

All Three Tenses

If you have difficulty fitting a verse into one of these categories, remember that it might be applicable to *all three* tenses. Here are a couple of examples:

*...you shall call His name Jesus, for He **will save** His people from their sins* (Mt. 1:21).

*In Him you also trusted, after you heard the word of truth, the gospel of your **salvation**; in whom also, having believed, you were sealed with the Holy Spirit of promise* (Eph. 1:13).

So in cases like these you don't have to choose, because they apply with equal force to all three phases of salvation.

2
Aspects of Justification

The New Testament teaches that we are justified by grace, by faith, by blood, by power, by works, and by God. This is apt to prove confusing, if not contradictory, unless we realize that in each case *a different aspect of the same subject is being presented.*

Justification Explained

First of all, what does *justification* mean? To *justify* means "to reckon righteous." It does not mean "to make righteous," but "to declare to be righteous." Actually it is a legal term; it comes from the courtroom.

We are not righteous in ourselves. We have no righteousness. But when we receive Jesus Christ as Lord and Savior, God reckons us to be righteous on the basis of Christ's substitutionary work. When we are "in Christ," God can righteously declare us to be righteous because full satisfaction has been made at Calvary for all our sins. The believing sinner is clothed in all the righteousness of God. "For He [God the Father] made Him [Christ] who knew no sin to be sin for us, that we might become the righteousness of God in Him" (2 Cor. 5:21).

As we mentioned at the outset, justification is said to be by grace, by faith, by blood, by power, by works, and by God.

How can it be by all of these six ways?

Justification by Grace

First, justification is *by grace.* In Romans 3:24 we read, "Being justified freely by His grace through the redemption that is in Christ Jesus." This means that man doesn't deserve to be justified. He can't merit it or earn it; he must receive it as a gift. Grace is the term upon which God gives justification to man—completely undeserved and unbought—freely, as a gift.

Justification by Faith

Second, justification is *by faith.* "Therefore, having been justified by faith, we have peace with God through our Lord Jesus Christ" (Rom. 5:1). This means that the sinner must receive justification by a definite act of trust in the Savior. Confessing himself to be worthy only of hell, he must accept the Lord Jesus as the One who paid the penalty of his sins on the Cross.

Grace is God stooping down to guilty man and offering justification as a free gift on the basis of Christ's redemptive work at Calvary. Faith is repentant man reaching up and receiving the gift from God without any thought of deserving it by his character or earning it by his works.

Justification by Blood

Justification is also *by blood.* "Much more then, having now been justified by His blood, we shall be saved from wrath through Him" (Rom. 5:9). This, of course, refers to the price which had to be paid in order that I might be justified. The sinless Savior shed His precious blood to settle the debt that my sins had accumulated. The enormous value of my justification is seen in the staggering price that was paid to secure it.

Justification by Power

While there is no Scripture that says in so many words that we are justified *by power,* the truth is contained in Romans 4:25: "[He] was delivered up because of our offenses, and was raised because of our justification." Here our justification is directly connected with the resurrection of Christ. And rightly so! If He had not risen, our faith would be futile, and we would still be in our sins (1 Cor. 15:17). So our justification is inseparably linked with the power that raised our Lord Jesus from the dead. That is why we can rightfully say that we are justified by power.

Justification by Works

We are justified *by works.* "You see then that a man is justified by works, and not by faith only" (Jas. 2:24). Here is where a distinct contradiction seems to appear. The apostle Paul teaches unmistakably that we are justified by faith alone. But James *seems* to say here, "Not so. We are justified by works." However, that is *not* what James is saying. He does not teach that justification is obtained initially by doing good works. Neither does he say that we are justified by faith plus works. What he is saying is that we are justified by *the kind of faith that results in a life of good works.*

It's futile for a person to *say* he has faith if he doesn't have works to back it up. People won't believe him. That kind of faith—that is, a faith of words only, is worthless (Jas. 2:14-17). True faith is invisible but can be demonstrated by works (Jas. 2:18). Abraham was justified by believing the Lord (Gen.

19

15:6), but years later he showed that his faith was genuine by being willing to offer his son Isaac as a burnt offering (Gen. 22:9-14). Rahab proved the reality of her faith by harboring the Israeli spies and helping them escape (Jas. 2:25). So when we speak of justification by works, we mean that works are the outward manifestation that we have truly been justified by faith. Works are not the cause; they are the *effect*. They are not the root; they are the *fruit* that justifies us before other people.

Justification by God

Finally, we are justified *by God:* "Who shall bring a charge against God's elect? It is God who justifies" (Rom. 8:33). He is the One who declares us righteous.

Summary

Putting these all together, we find that the New Testament teaches that we are justified by:

grace—this means we don't deserve it.
faith—this means we must receive it.
blood—this means it was purchased by the Savior's death.
power—this means that the Resurrection proves God's satisfaction with the Savior's work.
works—this means that when we are genuinely justified by faith, there will be good works to demonstrate it to others.
God—this means that He is the Justifier of the one who believes on Jesus.

All these aspects of justification have been expressed poetically as follows:

20

God's sovereign grace invited me
To have in heaven a place;
'Twas the good pleasure of His will;
I'm justified by grace.

In due time Christ on Calvary died;
There flowed that crimson flood
Which makes the foulest white as snow;
I'm justified by blood.

God raised Him up; this is the pledge,
Should evil doubtings lower;
His resurrection quells each fear;
I'm justified by power.

The Holy Spirit guided me
To what the Scripture saith;
I grasped the truth; Christ died for me!
I'm justified by faith.

Now if you doubt that I am Christ's,
If one suspicion lurks,
I'll show by deed that I am His;
I'm justified by works.

I praise the Lord, it's all of Him,
The grace, the faith, the blood,
The resurrection power, the works;
I'm justified by God!

—HELEN H. SHAW

3
Aspects of Eternal Life

A Quality of Life

Eternal life is not the same as endless existence. Everyone, saved and unsaved, will live forever, but only believers have eternal *life*. It's not only a *duration* of life but a *quality* as well. It's the life of God Himself, nothing less than union with God, and it's embodied in the Lord Jesus.

The life was manifested and we have seen, and bear witness, and declare to you that eternal life which was with the Father and was manifested to us (1 Jn. 1:2. See also 1 Jn. 5:20).

In his unfallen condition of innocence, Adam did not have eternal life. As long as he did not sin, he presumably would have continued to enjoy natural existence on earth, but he would not have had the hope of being glorified with Christ in heaven. And there was always the awful possibility that he would sin and thus be doomed to die—which is exactly what happened. It was not until he put His faith in the Lord as his Savior that he received eternal life, with all the everlasting blessings that it includes.

Sometimes everlasting[1] life is spoken of as a present possession, and at other times as a future hope and inheritance.

A Present Possession

It's a gift possessed by believers at the present time. The gift was promised by the Lord (1 Jn. 2:25), and is found in Him (Jn. 6:68; 1 Jn. 5:11). It's received by believing on Him:

Most assuredly, I say to you, He who believes in Me has everlasting life (Jn. 6:47. See also Jn. 3:15-16, 36; 5:24; 6:40; 1 Tim. 1:16).

Other expressions that mean the same as believing on Him are drinking the water He gives (Jn. 4:14); eating His flesh and drinking His blood (Jn. 6:54); following Him (Jn. 10:27); and knowing Him (Jn. 17:3). John says that no murderer has eternal life dwelling in him (1 Jn. 3:15), but he could just as well have said this about all other unbelieving sinners.

Eternal life is a gift from the Father (Rom. 6:23; 1 Jn. 5:11). Eternal life is also given by the Son.

27 My sheep hear My voice, and I know them, and they follow Me. 28 And I give them eternal life, and they shall never perish; neither shall anyone snatch them out of My hand (Jn. 10:27-28. See also Jn. 17:2).

All that the Father commanded Christ to speak had as its object the giving of eternal life (Jn. 12:50).

All who are ordained to eternal life believe (Acts 13:48); that is one side of the truth. The other is that those who refuse to believe thereby consider themselves unworthy of eternal life (Acts 13:46). This life is produced by the reign of grace (Rom. 5:21), and all who believe can know that they have it on the authority of the Word of God:

These things I have written to you who believe in the name of the Son of God, that you may know that you have eternal life, and that you may continue to believe in the name of the Son of God. (1 Jn. 5:13).

Those who have eternal life are expected to work it out practically from day to day.

Fight the good fight of faith, lay hold on eternal life, to which you were also called and have confessed the good confession in the presence of many witnesses (1 Tim. 6:12).

…Storing up for themselves a good foundation for the time to come, that they may lay hold on eternal life (1 Tim. 6:19. See also Jn. 6:27).

A Future Hope

In addition to being a present possession, eternal life is also spoken of in the future tense:

…In hope of eternal life which God, who cannot lie, promised before time began (Titus 1:2).

Keep yourselves in the love of God, looking for the mercy of our Lord Jesus Christ unto eternal life (Jude 21).

This refers to eternal life in its fullness, when the believer will be forever free from sin, sickness, sorrow, and death. It refers to the final, glorified state.

Sometimes eternal life is spoken of in terms of an inheritance:

And everyone who has left houses or brothers or sisters or father or mother or wife or children or lands, for My name's sake, shall receive a hundredfold, and inherit eternal life (Mt. 19:29. See also Mk 10:29-30; Lk 18:30).

25

...That having been justified by His grace we should become heirs according to the hope of eternal life (Titus 3:7).

Not Earned by Works

There are other verses that sound as if eternal life is a reward for a person's behavior on earth. Verses that fall into this category are Matthew 25:45-46; Luke 18:29-30; John 4:36; 12:25; Romans 2:7; Galatians 6:8. However, these few verses cannot contradict the many passages that teach the great truth that salvation is by grace, that it's a gift, that it is received by faith alone, and that it is completely apart from works.

So what do these troublesome verses mean? They remind us that there will be degrees of *reward* in heaven. At the Judgment Seat of Christ, some will receive crowns, others will suffer loss. Although all believers will have eternal life, not all will have the same capacity for enjoying it (1 Cor. 15:41b). That is determined down here by faithfulness in service (Gal. 6:7-9) and progress in holiness (Rom. 6:22).

The good works that are mentioned in these verses are the fruit of a person's eternal life, not the way by which he obtains it. For example, when it says in Matthew 25:46, "And these will go away into everlasting punishment, but the righteous into eternal life," it teaches that those who befriend Christ's Jewish brethren during the Tribulation Period will show by this that they are truly saved, and will thus enjoy eternal life. Their good works are the evidence of their salvation.

John 4:36 and 12:25 clearly refer to the rewards for faithful service, not to the way of salvation.

36 And he who reaps receives wages, and gathers fruit for eternal life, that both he who sows and he who reaps may rejoice together.

26

25 He who loves his life will lose it, and he who hates his life in this world will keep it for eternal life.

Romans 2:7 is a verse that is especially difficult for many.

...Eternal life to those who by patient continuance in doing good seek for glory, honor, and immortality.

On the face of it, this seems to say that eternal life is conditioned on being or doing good. The consistent testimony of Scripture forbids this interpretation. There are two ways in which it may be biblically understood. First, it is a *theoretical* ideal, a standard by which God will judge the lost. If an unbeliever *could* prove that, by his own strength, he continued without exception in well-doing, he would be awarded eternal life. But, of course, this is impossible. "There is none who does good, no, not one" (Rom. 3:12c). Or it may be that only a believer, by the power of the Holy Spirit, can meet this description. And in that case, of course, good works are the outcome of salvation, not its source.

Summary

Eternal life is a spiritual life received by the new birth. It's the life of God Himself and as eternal as He is. It's a present possession and a future hope. A person who truly believes on Christ can know that he has it on the authority of the Word of God. *Assurance of salvation comes through the Scriptures.*

The believer looks forward to eternal life in its fullness, otherwise known as the redemption of the body.

When eternal life is spoken of in connection with rewards, it can't mean that it is the reward for holiness, service, or good works. Rewards are given for a faithful demonstration that the life of Christ in a believer makes a difference.

Endnote

1. *Everlasting* and *eternal* in the King James tradition both translate the same Greek word, *aionios*. The two words are used for literary variety and no attempt should be made to make them say different things.

4
Atonement Then & Now

Atonement is one of those fascinating Bible words with a variety of usages. The significance of the word in any particular verse of Scripture must be determined by the context. We learn the meanings of the word by its usage.

But before we get to that, let us remind ourselves of the way of salvation in the Old Testament. People were saved when they put their faith in the Lord. When God made a revelation to them and they believed Him, they were reckoned righteous. Thus when God promised Abraham that he would have descendants as numerous as the stars, the patriarch "believed in the Lord, and He accounted it to him for righteousness" (Gen. 15:6). Abraham was justified on the basis of the still-future work of Christ. It is doubtful that Abraham knew very much about that work, but God knew about it, and put all the value of it to Abraham's account. The Lord granted him judicial forgiveness of all his sins on the basis of the Savior's precious blood shed on Calvary. Salvation in every age is by faith in the Lord and on the basis of the substitutionary work of the Lord Jesus. An everlasting relationship is established.

However, sins which a believing Israelite committed following his conversion broke his fellowship with God and made him unclean. Also there were certain acts (like touching a dead body) which, although not sinful, made him ceremonially defiled. These things barred him from worshipping at the tabernacle or temple. This was where atonement was needed, so let us now turn to consider this subject.

The Old Testament Meaning

In the Old Testament, atonement translates a Hebrew word meaning "covering."[1] Thus when God told Noah to cover the ark inside and out with tar, He used the same root word translated "to atone." Atonement was a covering of sin until it was dealt with completely, perfectly, and finally by the work of Christ on Calvary.

In some places, to *atone* may have the idea of to make amends, to cleanse, to exempt from punishment, and to consecrate.

The word was generally used of people, of priests, and of the nation of Israel. But almost never did it signify expiation of sins, that is, making satisfaction for them. The writer to the Hebrews makes it clear that the Old Testament sacrifices never removed a single sin. If the primary meaning of atonement is the putting away of sin, then the sacrifices were failures. "For it is not possible that the blood of bulls and goats could take away sins" (Heb. 10:4). On the Day of Atonement, there was an annual remembrance of sins (Heb. 10:3). For that reason, the sacrificial system never gave the people of God a clear conscience with regard to sins. "For then would they not have ceased to be offered? For the worshippers, once purified, would have had no more consciousness of sins" (Heb. 10:2).

Atonement was sometimes made for inanimate things—the altar, the holy place, the most holy place, the tabernacle of meeting, and the temple. Obviously this had nothing to do with putting away or expiation of sins, since inanimate things cannot sin. An altar for which atonement had been made was an altar that was thus made fit to be used for divine service because it was ritually clean. Any definition of atonement that fails to explain why certain "things" had to be atoned for is inadequate.

When used of persons, atonement had to do with ceremonial cleansing. When a believing Jew had sinned and then brought the required sacrifice, he was, in effect, confessing his sin. As soon as he confessed, he was forgiven. His forgiveness did not come through an animal sacrifice but through the sacrifice of Christ, which it typified. The eternal penalty of his sin had already been cancelled when he believed in the Lord, but confession renewed his fellowship with God. The sacrifice he brought provided an outward, ceremonial fitness for him to participate in the worship and service of Jehovah again. He was already in covenant relation with God, but he was now ritually clean. The Levitical sacrifices sanctified to the purifying of the flesh,[2] that is, they provided a ritual, outward purification. Only the work of Christ could purge the conscience from dead works to serve the living God.[3]

One Exception to the Rule

There is at least one place in the Old Testament where the word atone can clearly mean to *put away sin:*

Seventy weeks are determined for your people and for your holy city, to finish the transgression, to make an end of sins, to make reconciliation for iniquity, to bring in everlasting righteousness, to seal up vision and prophecy, and to anoint the Most Holy (Dan. 9:24).

In this verse, the expression *to make reconciliation for iniquity* is literally *to atone for wickedness* (it is so translated in the

31

NASB and the NIV). The translators of the KJV and the NKJV apparently wanted to avoid any suggestion that the work of Christ merely provided covering for sins and so they translated it *to make reconciliation for iniquity.*

The passage points forward to the Second Coming of the Lord Jesus when the wickedness of His people Israel will be finally settled. Actually the necessary sacrifice was offered at Calvary, but Israel as a whole will not reap the benefit of it until they look on Him whom they pierced and mourn for Him as one mourns for an only son (see Zech. 12:10; Jn. 19:37). What atonement covered in the Old Testament, Christ dealt with fully and finally at the Cross.

The Acquired Meaning

Atonement is not a New Testament word. The Old Testament idea of atonement is never found in the New Testament. There is never a mention of covering being made for people or for inanimate things. (In the KJV, the word is found in Romans 5:11, but the proper translation there is *reconciliation.*[4] Practically all the modern translations have dropped *atonement* in favor of *reconciliation.*)

In our day, the word atonement has an acquired meaning. We speak of the atonement of Christ, meaning the satisfaction that has been made for sins through His death, burial, and resurrection. In sermon and song, we rejoice that through His atoning blood our sins have been put away once for all. But this meaning is entirely a matter of usage, and has no connection with the usual meaning of the word in the Old Testament.

It will save a lot of confusion and misunderstanding if we distinguish between the Old Testament meaning of atonement and the meaning it has acquired today through usage. It is not wrong to speak of the atoning work of Christ as long as we realize that His work was perfect, final, and inward, whereas atonement in the Old Testament was, with at least one exception, imperfect, repeated, and outward.

Atonement in the Kingdom

The word is used by Ezekiel in connection with the services of the future millennial temple.[5] Looking forward to the kingdom, Ezekiel speaks of atonement being made for the altar, for the people, *i.e.*, the house of Israel, and for the temple. This has posed a problem for some. It seems to contradict Hebrews 10:12, "But this Man, after He had offered one sacrifice for sins forever, sat down at the right hand of God," and Hebrews 10:18, "Now where there is remission of these, there is no longer an offering for sin."

The problem arises because we give the word *atonement* the modern dictionary meaning rather than its basic meaning. There is no suggestion that the sacrifices at the millennial temple will be any more effective in removing the guilt and penalty of sins than they were in the Old Testament era. They will be merely a part of the temple ritual. In going through the ceremonies, redeemed Israel will see the weakness of the rituals when contrasted with the perfection of the work of Christ. They will realize that the ceremonies were shadows whereas the reality is Christ. Just as the atoning sacrifices of the Old Testament pointed forward to the work of Christ, so those of the millennium will point back to Calvary, as the Lord's Supper does for us. They will be memorials.

Endnotes

1. The verb is *kāphar,* which just coincidentally sounds like its English counterpart, cover. The noun form occurs in the still current name of the Jewish holiday, *Yom Kippur*, literally "Day of Covering" (*i.e.*, Atonement).

2. Hebrews 9:13.

3. Hebrews 9:14.

4. The noun *katallage* used here is the standard Greek word for "reconciliation."

5. Ezekiel 43:20, 26; 45:15, 17, 20.

Part II

DISTINCTIONS IN THE CHRISTIAN LIFE

5
Position & Practice

There is no key more helpful in unlocking the New Testament than an understanding of the difference between the believer's *position* and his *practice*. If you don't see this distinction, there will be times when passages will be positively confusing and even seemingly contradictory.

Position and practice are sometimes spoken of as *standing* and *state*; the meaning is the same. In brief, a Christian's position is his standing in Christ—what he is in Christ. His practice is what he is in himself—or better, what he *should be*. The first has to do with *doctrine,* the second with *duty.* The first is *fact,* the second is *experience.* The first is *union,* the second is *communion.*

There's a difference between what a believer is in Christ and what he is in himself. Grace has given the person in Christ an absolutely perfect standing before God. He is accepted in the Beloved One (Eph. 1:6) and complete in Christ (Col. 2:10). His sins have been forgiven and he is clothed in all the righteousness of God (2 Cor. 5:21). It is no presumption for him to say:

> *Near, so very near to God,*
> *I could not nearer be;*
> *For in the Person of God's Son*
> *I am as near as He.*

Dear, so very dear to God,
Dearer I could not be;
The love with which He loves His Son,
That is His love to me. —CATESBY PAGET

The believer's practice is something else again. Unfortunately, it's far from perfect! In most cases it varies from day to day. Sometimes the believer is on the mountaintop spiritually. At other times he may be in the valley of defeat.

Now God's will is that our practice should increasingly correspond to our position. Out of love for the One who died for us, our everyday lives should be constantly growing in Christlikeness. As Phillips Brooks, the author of the beloved American Christmas carol, "O Little Town of Bethlehem," said, "Christianity knows no truth that is not the parent of duty." Of course, we will never reach a perfect state in this life; that will never happen until we die or until the Savior returns. But the process should be going on; we should be becoming in practice more and more like what we are in position.

When we see the Savior we will be automatically like Him (1 Jn. 3:2). This transformation will take place by divine power, without any cooperation on our part. But it brings more glory to God if His people are growing in the likeness of the Lord Jesus in this life, not to mention its being a much better "advertisement" for the truth of the Christian faith.

Distinguishing Position and Practice

How can you tell whether a particular passage is speaking about our position or our practice? Well, watch for such phrases as "in Christ," "in the Beloved," or "in Him." When you find such phrases, you can usually be sure that the writer is speaking about our position (see Eph. 1:3-14). The best way to identify our practice is to notice when we find a verse that tells us *what we ought to be or do.*

The invariable order you will find in the New Testament is position first, then practice. Several of the Epistles are structured on this order. In Ephesians, for instance, the first three chapters describe what we *are* in Christ; the last three describe what we *should be* in daily living. In the first three chapters we find ourselves in heavenly places in Christ; in the last three we are tackling the nitty-gritty problems of the home and the workaday world.

Examples of Differences

Now let's see how helpful it is to be aware of this distinction as we study the New Testament. Here are seven simple examples of the difference between position and practice.

Example 1:

Position	Practice
For by one offering He has perfected forever those who are being sanctified.	*Therefore you shall be perfect, just as your Father in heaven is perfect.*
(Heb. 10:14)	(Mt. 5:48)

The first verse says that all believers *are* perfect; the second says that all believers *should be* perfect. This would sound like doubletalk if we didn't realize that the first speaks of our standing and the second of our state.

Example 2:

Position	Practice
...How shall we who died to sin live any longer in it?	*Likewise you also, reckon yourselves to be dead indeed to sin.*
(Rom. 6:2)	(Rom. 6:11a)

39

You *are* dead to sin—this is the position into which grace has put you. Now *be* dead to sin day by day—this is what your practice should be.

Example 3:

Position	*Practice*
But as many as received Him, to them He gave the right to become children of God, to those who believe in His name. (Jn. 1:12)	*Therefore be imitators of God as dear children.* (Eph. 5:1)

As soon as a person is born again he becomes a child of God. From then on he should be an imitator of God as a beloved child. All who are God's children are expected to bear the family likeness, that is, to be godly.

Example 4:

Position	*Practice*
God is faithful, by whom you were called into the fellowship of His Son, Jesus Christ our Lord. (1 Cor. 1:9)	*I...beseech you to walk worthy of the calling with which you were called.* (Eph. 4:1)

We've been called to a wonderful fellowship. Privilege carries responsibility. We should walk worthy of our calling.

Example 5:

Position	*Practice*
To all who are in Rome, beloved of God, called to be saints. (Rom. 1:7)	*...Receive her in the Lord in a manner worthy of the saints.* (Rom. 16:2)

Paul addresses the Christians in Rome as "saints"; they were "set apart" ones. If they were saved, they were saints. But saints should be saintly; this is the practical side of it, as brought out in Romans 16:2.

Example 6:

Position	Practice
For by grace you have been saved through faith... (Eph. 2:8a)	*...Work out your own salvation with fear and trembling* (Phil. 2:12b)

Our standing is a gift from God. Our state is the way we should express our gratitude. Notice that the standing always comes first, then the state. We don't become Christians by living the Christian life. Rather, we live the Christian life because we've become Christians.

Example 7:

Position	Practice
Through whom also we have access by faith into this grace in which we stand... (Rom. 5:2a)	*But I trust in the Lord Jesus to send Timothy to you shortly, that I also may be encouraged when I know your state* (Phil. 2:19)

The grace in which we stand is our position of favor in Christ. Our state is the condition of our daily conduct as believers.

Example 8:

As a final example, we will take Colossians 3:1-5 and show

41

how Paul alternates between position and practice.

Position	Practice
If then you were raised with Christ... (v. 1).	*...Seek those things which are above, where Christ is, sitting at the right hand of God* (v. 1).
	Set your mind on things above, not on things on the earth (v. 2).
For you died, and your life is hidden with Christ in God (v. 3).	*Therefore put to death your members which are on the earth...* (v. 5a).

Paul is saying, in effect, "You *are dead*; now *be dead*. You *are risen*; now *live the resurrection life*." What would otherwise be unintelligible becomes clear when we realize that the apostle is speaking about what we are in Christ on one hand, and what we should be in ourselves on the other.

A Personal Illustration

In closing, please allow me to illustrate how the distinction between standing and state helped me through a difficult period in my life. After I was saved, I used to hear people quote 2 Corinthians 5:17 when they gave their testimony: "Therefore, if anyone is in Christ, he is a new creation; old things have passed away; behold, all things have become new."

They would tell of the wonderful transformation that had taken place in their lives—how *all* the old things had passed away and *all* things had become new. I would sit there and think, "I wish I could say that all the old things had passed away in *my* life, and that all things had become new." But it wasn't so. I still had some of the old habits, some evil thoughts, displays of anger, and many other graveclothes from my pre-converted days. At times I doubted my salvation.

Then one day I noticed the phrase "in Christ," and my heart leaped with joy. I realized that the verse was talking about my position—not my practice. And of course "in Christ," it *was* all true. In Him all the old things had *indeed* passed away—condemnation, the dominion of Satan, the fear of death, and so forth. In Him everything was new—forgiveness, acceptance, justification, sanctification, and a host of other blessings. From that time on, this verse has held no terror for me. I love it. And the knowledge of what I am in Christ makes me want to live for Him as the Lord of my life.

Question: Standing and state are found in 1 Corinthians 5:7, Ephesians 5:8, and 1 Peter 2:9. Can you identify them?

6
Relationship & Fellowship

This study is somewhat similar to the one on position and practice. But the difference is important enough to devote a separate chapter to it.

Relationship with God

When a person is born again, a new relationship is formed; he or she becomes a child of God.

But as many as received Him, to them He gave the right to become children of God, to those who believe in His name (Jn. 1:12).

Beloved, now we are children of God; and it has not yet been revealed what we shall be, but we know that when He is revealed, we shall be like Him, for we shall see Him as He is (1 Jn. 3:2).

Now there's something very final about a birth! Did you ever think about that? Once a birth has taken place, it lasts forever. You can't go back and undo it. A relationship is formed that can't be altered. Let's say, for example, that a son has just been born to the Joneses. No matter what happens, the child will always be a son of Mr. and Mrs. Jones, and they will always be his parents. In later life he may dishonor his family and cause them deepest grief. But the relationship still stands—Mr. Jones is still his father, and he is still the Joneses' son.

Now apply this to the believer. Through the new birth a relationship is formed with God the Father:

> *The Spirit Himself bears witness with our spirit that we are children of God* (Rom. 8:16).

> *Therefore you are no longer a slave but a son, and if a son, then an heir of God through Christ* (Gal. 4:7).

It's a relationship that can't be broken. Once a son or daughter, always a son or daughter.

Fellowship with God

But there's another side to the truth, and that side is fellowship. Our word *fellowship* translates a well-known Greek word, *koinonia*, which means sharing things in common. If relationship is *union*, then fellowship is *communion*. And if relationship is a chain that can't be broken, fellowship is a slender thread that is *very easily* broken.

Sin breaks fellowship with God. Two can't walk together unless they're agreed (Amos 3:3), and God can't walk in fellowship with His children when they sin: "God is light and in Him is no darkness at all" (1 Jn. 1:5b). He can't enjoy communion with those who are trying to cover up evil in their lives.

When fellowship is broken, the believer loses his or her joy, song, power for service, testimony, and effective prayer life.

Fellowship remains broken as long as sin is unconfessed and unforsaken. And broken fellowship is *very serious*. For example, a decision could be made when a believer is out of touch with the Lord that could put a blight on the rest of his life. How many backslidden Christians have chosen an unbelieving mate and ruined their lives as far as usefulness for God is concerned! Their *souls* are saved but their *lives* have been lost.

Broken fellowship brings the chastening, or discipline, of God. While a believer is free from the eternal punishment of sins, he's *not* free from the consequences of sin in his life. Why were some of the Corinthian saints sick? Because they were going to the communion table without first confessing their sins and straightening things out (1 Cor. 11:29-32). Some of them had even died. They had been made fit for heaven through the redemption that is in Christ Jesus, but they were unfit for further life and testimony here on earth.

Broken fellowship will result in loss of reward at the Judgment Seat of Christ (1 Cor. 3:15). All time spent out of fellowship with God is time forever wasted.

So while we rejoice in the truth that our relationship with God is unbreakable, we should greatly fear anything that breaks fellowship with our Father. Actually the knowledge that grace has brought us into such a wonderful relationship should be the strongest motive to maintain continuous communion with the Lord. Grace does *not* encourage sin; it is the most powerful deterrent to it.

Biblical Illustrations

In the Old Testament, David is a classic example of a saint whose fellowship with God was broken by sin. We read of his confession and restoration to the Lord in Psalms 32 and 51.

In the New Testament, the prodigal son may be taken as an illustration of a returning backslider (Lk. 15:11-24), though the story is commonly interpreted as the conversion of a sinner. Fellowship was broken through the son's waywardness and rebellion. But he was still a son, even in the far country. As soon as he returned and began to blurt out his confession, fellowship was restored. His father ran out, fell on his neck, and kissed him.

In 1 John 2:1 we read, "My little children, these things I write to you, so that you may not sin. And if anyone sins, we have an Advocate with the Father, Jesus Christ the righteous." This is written to *children,* to those who have been born into the family of God. (The word translated "little children" [*teknia*] literally means "little born ones," like the Scots word *bairnies.*) God's ideal is that His children should not sin. But we *do* sin, and God has made provision if anyone does sin: "we have an Advocate with the Father." Notice this—"we have an Advocate *with the Father.*" He's still our Father, even when we sin. How can that be? Because relationship is a tie that can never be broken. What happens when we sin? "We have an Advocate *with the Father,* Jesus Christ the righteous." He immediately goes to work in our lives, bringing us to the place where we are willing to confess and forsake our sins, thus enjoying the Father's fellowship once more.

When I see the difference between relationship and fellowship, it helps me understand these Scriptures. It also makes me appreciate the eternal security I have in Christ and motivates me to live in fellowship with my Father who loves me so.

7
Judicial & Parental Forgiveness

Two different kinds of forgiveness are found in God's Word, and if we are going to be careful students of Scripture, we must learn to distinguish them. We will call them *judicial* and *parental* forgiveness (though these names themselves are not used in the Bible).

Definitions

To put it very simply, judicial forgiveness is the forgiveness of a *judge,* and parental forgiveness is the forgiveness of a *father.* The first term is taken from the *courtroom* and the second from the *home.*

Judicial Forgiveness

First let's go to the courtroom. God is the Judge and sinful man is the person on trial. Man is guilty of sinning, and the penalty is eternal death. But the Lord Jesus appears and announces, "I will pay the penalty which man's sins deserved; I will die as a Substitute for him!" This is what the Savior did on the Cross of Calvary. Now the Judge announces to sinful man, "If you will accept my Son as your Lord and Savior, I will forgive you." As soon as the man puts his faith in the Savior, he receives judicial forgiveness of all his sins. He will never have to pay the punishment for them in hell, because Christ has paid it all. The forgiven sinner now enters into a new relationship: God is no longer his Judge; He is now his Father.

Parental Forgiveness

So now we move to the home for an illustration of parental forgiveness. God is the Father and the believer is the child. In an unguarded moment, the child commits an act of sin. Then what happens? Does God sentence the child to die for the sin? Of course not! Why not? Because God is no longer the Judge, but the Father! What *does* happen? Well, fellowship within the family is broken. The happy family spirit is gone. The child hasn't lost his salvation, but he *has* lost the *joy* of his salvation. Soon he may experience his Father's discipline, designed to bring him back into fellowship. As soon as the child confesses his sin, he receives parental forgiveness.

Judicial forgiveness takes place once-for-all at the time of conversion; parental forgiveness takes place every time a believer confesses and forsakes his sin. This is what Jesus taught in John 13:8-10. We need the *bath* of regeneration only once to deliver us from the penalty of sins, but we need many *cleansings* throughout our Christian lives to give us parental forgiveness.

The Two Types Differentiated

The difference between the two types of forgiveness may be summarized graphically as follows:

	Judicial	**Parental**
The Person's Status	Sinner *(Rom. 3:23)*	Child *(1 John 3:2)*
Relationship of God	Judge *(Ps. 96:13)*	Father *(Gal. 4:6)*
Result of sin	Eternal death *(Rom. 6:23)*	Broken fellowship *(1 John 1:6)*
Role of Christ	Savior *(1 Tim. 1:15)*	High Priest and Advocate *(Heb. 4:14-16; 1 Jn. 2:1)*
The Person's Need	Salvation *(Acts 16:30)*	Joy of salvation *(Ps. 51:12)*
Means of Forgiveness	Faith *(Acts 16:31)*	Confession *(1 Jn. 1:9)*
Kind of Forgiveness	Judicial *(Rom. 8:1)*	Parental *(Lk. 15:21-22)*
Consequence Averted	Hell *(Jn. 5:24)*	Chastening *(1 Cor. 11:31-32)* Loss of reward at the Judgment Seat of Christ *(1 Cor. 3:15)*
Positive Result	New relationship *(Jn. 1:12)*	Renewed fellowship *(Ps. 32:5)*
Frequency	Once for all (one bath of regeneration) *(Jn. 13:10)*	Many times (many cleansings) *(Jn. 13:8)*

Scriptures on Judicial Forgiveness

From now on, when we come to verses that speak about the once-for-all forgiveness that is granted to us as sinners through the work of Christ, we'll know that the subject is *judicial* forgiveness. The following illustrate this:

In Him we have redemption through His blood, the forgiveness of sins, according to the riches of His grace (Eph. 1:7).

And be kind to one another, tenderhearted, forgiving one another, even as God in Christ forgave you (Eph. 4:32).

And you, being dead in your trespasses and the uncircumcision of your flesh, He has made alive together with Him, having forgiven you all trespasses (Col. 2:13).

Scriptures on Parental Forgiveness

However, there are other passages of Scripture that deal with *parental* forgiveness:

14 For if you forgive men their trespasses, your heavenly Father will also forgive you. 15 But if you do not forgive men their trespasses, neither will your Father forgive your trespasses (Mt. 6:14-15).

Judge not, and you shall not be judged. Condemn not, and you shall not be condemned. Forgive, and you will be forgiven (Lk. 6:37).

And whenever you stand praying, if you have anything against anyone, forgive him, that your Father in heaven may also forgive you your trespasses (Mk. 11:25).

Notice that in three of these verses God is specifically

called *Father*: it's the *Father's* forgiveness that is involved. Notice also that our being forgiven depends on our willingness to forgive others. That's not true of judicial forgiveness; willingness to forgive others is not a condition of eternal salvation. But it is true of parental forgiveness; our Father will not forgive us if we don't forgive one another.

In Matthew 18:23-35, Jesus told the story of a slave who had been forgiven 10,000 talents (an enormous sum!) by the king. But that same slave wouldn't forgive one of his fellow-slaves 100 denarii (a not-too-large debt). So the king was furious with him and delivered him to the jailers till he paid his whole debt. Jesus concluded the parable by saying, "So My heavenly Father also will do to you if each of you, from his heart, does not forgive his brother his trespasses" (v. 35). Here again it's a matter of the Father's forgiveness. It's sin to have an unforgiving spirit, and God can't forgive us parentally until we confess that sin and forsake it.

One of the thrills of Bible study is to see these basic distinctions and to be able to apply them in our daily reading. From now on when you come to the subject of forgiveness in the Word, you should be able to say, "Oh, yes, that refers to judicial forgiveness," or else, "That must refer to the Father's forgiveness of His child." Just remember: The sinner receives *judicial* forgiveness when he believes on the Lord Jesus Christ; the believer receives *paternal* or *parental* forgiveness when he confesses his sins.

8
The Two Natures

In discussing biblical distinctions, none is more practical than the difference between the believer's two natures. When a Christian is unaware of this truth, he is apt to be torn by guilt, doubt, and discouragement. So it is important to realize that every Christian has two natures, an old one and a new one, and to understand the characteristics of each.

The Old Nature

Everyone, saved and unsaved, has an old nature. It is the only one an unbeliever has. It is inherited from Adam and remains throughout life. We may call it the Adam nature, the old man, or the flesh. David acknowledged it in these words: "Behold, I was brought forth in iniquity, and in sin my mother conceived me" (Ps. 51:5). Paul was referring to it when he wrote, "For I know that in me (that is, in my flesh) nothing good dwells" (Rom. 7:18a). We should not look for anything good in it, and should not be disappointed when we don't find it. It is sobering to realize that each of us has a nature that is capable of any sin in the book.

The Adam nature is one of the believer's three enemies, the other two being the world and the Devil. The old nature is the enemy within, the quisling or fifth columnist. It loves to feed on what is unedifying and unclean. It accounts for man's natural bent against God. It harbors enmity against God, is not subject to the law of God, and cannot please God. Because of it, people are more inclined to accept error rather than truth.

The Adam nature is incurably evil. Even when a man or woman has lived a holy life for many years, the old nature is no better. The Lord is not in the business of improving or reforming it. He condemned it at the cross of Calvary. "God [sent] His own Son in the likeness of sinful flesh, and on account of sin, condemned sin in the flesh" (Rom. 8:3). "Our old man was crucified with Him" (Rom. 6:6). Now God instructs the believer to reckon it to be dead, that is, to respond to it as a dead person would.

When a person is forbidden to do something, the old nature immediately wants to do it. Paul describes this weird experience in Romans 7:7c-9):

> 7...*For I would not have known covetousness, unless the law had said, "You shall not covet." 8 But sin, taking opportunity by the commandment, produced in me all manner of evil desires. For apart from the law sin was dead. 9 I was alive once without the law, but when the commandment came, sin revived and I died.*

Paul also likened the old nature to a dead body that was strapped to his back. The picture, of course, is of a decaying, foul-smelling corpse. It followed him everywhere, causing him to cry out in anguish, "O wretched man that I am! Who will deliver me from this body of death?" (Rom. 7:24).

The old nature is what we are in Adam. The Lord Jesus died for that just as well as for sins that we have committed. That is a comfort, because what we are is a lot worse than anything we have ever done.

All that we have said does not deny the fact that unbelievers can often be kind, compassionate, loving, and generous. This behavior may be accounted for in several ways. It may be natural instinct, *e.g.*, the love of a mother for her baby. It may be a matter of impulse, or a learned behavior. It may be due to the influence of Christianity, which is salt and light in the world. And it may be motivated by the desire to earn or deserve salvation. Whatever the source, one thing is certain. The first truly good work that any unsaved person can do is to trust in Christ (Jn. 6:39).

The New Nature

When a person is born again, he or she receives a new nature, a divine nature (2 Pet. 1:4), the life of Christ. This nature cannot sin because it is born of God (1 Jn. 3:9).

It is good and capable only of what is good. We may call it the Christ nature or the new man.

It likes to feed on what is pure and holy. It responds eagerly to the Word of God. It delights in the law of the Lord. His commandments are not burdensome; they are the very things that the new nature loves to do. They are like commanding a mother to take good care of her baby; that is exactly what she wants to do.

The two natures may be compared to the raven and dove which Noah released from the ark. The raven never returned; it was satisfied to feed on all the decaying flesh that was floating on the water. The dove, representing the new nature, returned to the ark until it could find a clean place on which to rest and feed.

How true the words of the Lord Jesus, "That which is born of the flesh is flesh, and that which is born of the Spirit is spirit" (Jn. 3:6).

The Fight is On!

A new convert had a colorful way of describing his dual condition. He said, "Sin was taken out of my heart, but my grandfather is still in my bones."

As soon as a person is saved, the two natures begin to fight against one another. It is not surprising. How could two natures, so diametrically different, live at peace? The battle is pictured by the two babies that struggled in Rebekah's womb (Gen. 25:22-23). She asked, "If all is well, why am I this way?" Paul describes the conflict in living color in Romans 7:14-25:

14 *For we know that the law is spiritual, but I am carnal, sold under sin.* 15 *For what I am doing, I do not understand. For what I will to do, that I do not practice; but what I hate, that I do.* 16 *If then I do what I will not to do, I agree with the law that it is good.* 17 *But now it is no longer I that do it, but sin that dwells in me.* 18 *For I know that in me (that is, in my flesh), nothing good dwells; for to will is present with me, but how to perform what is good I do not find.* 19 *For the good that I will to do, I do not do; but the evil I will not to do, that I practice.* 20 *Now if I do what I will not to do, it is no longer I who do it, but sin that dwells in me.* 21 *I find then a law, that evil is present with me; the one who wills to do good.* 22 *For I delight in the law of God according to the inward man.* 23 *But I see another law in my members, warring against the law of my mind, and bringing me into captivity to the law of sin which is in my members.* 24 *O wretched man that I am! Who will deliver me from this body of death?* 25 *I thank God—through Jesus Christ our Lord! So then, with the mind I myself serve the law of God, but with the flesh the law of sin.*

A picture of a conflict that is related but not identical is the battle between the flesh and the Holy Spirit (Gal. 5:17):

For the flesh lusts against the Spirit, and the Spirit against the flesh; and these are contrary to one another, so that you do not do the things that you wish.

No wonder a believer often feels that he is schizophrenic, a split personality, a Dr. Jekyll and Mr. Hyde. No wonder that, like Rebekah, he is puzzled by this inward conflict. He thought (correctly) that the battle would be over when he trusted the Lord, but now he finds that another fierce war has begun, and he is dismayed. He might even doubt his salvation.

He should know that every Christian, even the most saintly, has this battle (1 Cor. 10:13), and that it will continue until death or the Rapture. Instead of being evidence that he isn't saved, it is more likely to be confirmation that he really is.

Which Nature Wins?

The Holy Spirit is the One who gives deliverance from the power of indwelling sin (Gal. 5:17). The godliest believer does not have that power in himself. However, the obedience and cooperation of the Christian are necessary.

The believer is the one who determines which nature wins. It is the nature he feeds. He can't feed the flesh with TV, movies, and worldly literature and entertainment, and expect the new nature to come out on top. He can't feed the wolf and expect the lamb to win.

That is why he is told in Romans 13:14 to "make no provision for the flesh, to fulfill its lusts" and in 1 Peter 2:11 to "abstain from fleshly lusts which war against the soul."

On the positive side, he is obligated to spend much time in

the Word, in prayer, and in service for the Lord. All the actions that make for a life of holiness are required.

No Excuses, Please!

We mustn't excuse our sinning by passing the buck to the old nature. That is a form of blame-shifting that will not work. God holds the *person* responsible, not the nature.

Excusing sin makes it easier to commit. It lowers one's resistance.

Conclusion

Both the Bible and our experience tell us that we have two natures. They might be called by different names, but they are there nonetheless. If a believer doesn't see this, he might feel like a contradiction. Or he might question the validity of his conversion. Or he might live a defeated life.

The solution of his predicament lies in responding to the evil desires of the old nature like a dead man would, and in submitting himself to the control of the Holy Spirit. As long as he does this, he will not fulfill the lusts of the flesh (Gal. 5:16).

9
Kinds of Sanctification

The word *sanctify* means "to set apart." There is a whole family of words—*sanctify, sanctification, saint, holy, holiness, consecrate, consecration*—that all have the same root meaning. Very often sanctification means the process of separating from common or unclean uses to divine service. But not always. If you just remember that to sanctify means to set apart, you will have a definition that fits *all* cases.

In the Old Testament God sanctified the seventh day (Gen. 2:3). The firstborn of both men and animals were sanctified to the Lord (Ex. 13:2). The priests were told to consecrate themselves to the Lord (Ex. 19:22). Mt. Sinai was sanctified (Ex. 19:23). The Tabernacle and all its furniture were sanctified (Ex. 40:9). In Isaiah 66:17, we read that the people sanctified themselves to worship idols.

In the New Testament, *sanctification* is used primarily in regard to people. However, Jesus said that the Temple sanctifies the gold on it, and that the altar sanctifies the gift on it (Mt. 23:17, 19). Paul taught that when we give thanks for our food, it is consecrated by the Word of God and prayer (1 Tim. 4:5).

With regard to the sanctification of persons, God consecrated Christ and sent Him into the world (Jn. 10:36); that is, the Father set His Son apart for the work of saving us from our sins. Jesus consecrated Himself (Jn. 17:19); in other words, He set Himself apart in order to intercede for His people.

There is a sense in which even certain *unbelievers* are sanctified: "For the unbelieving husband is sanctified by the wife, and the unbelieving wife is sanctified by the husband" (1 Cor. 7:14a). This means that the unbelieving partner is set apart in a position of privilege by having a Christian spouse praying for his or her salvation.

And there is a sense in which Christ should be sanctified by all believers. "But sanctify the Lord God in your hearts..." (1 Pet. 3:15). We sanctify Him by setting Him apart as undisputed Sovereign in our lives.

In addition to the above, however, there are four other important kinds of sanctification which we should distinguish in our study of the New Testament. These are called *preconversion* sanctification, *positional* sanctification, *progressive* sanctification, and *perfect* sanctification.

Pre-Conversion Sanctification

Long before a person is born again, the Holy Spirit has been working in his life, setting him apart from the world and wooing him to Christ. Paul realized that he had been set apart before he was born (Gal. 1:15). In 2 Thessalonians 2:13, the apostle reminds the Thessalonians that there were three steps in their salvation:

1. Their selection by God.
2. Their sanctification by the Spirit.
3. Their belief in the truth.

Notice that this sanctification was *before* they believed and were saved.

In 1 Peter 1:2, the order of events connected with salvation is linked as follows:

1. Choice by God the Father.
2. Sanctification by the Spirit.
3. Obedience to Jesus Christ.
4. Sprinkling with His blood.

In eternity God chose us in Christ (see Eph. 1:4). In time the Holy Spirit set us apart. Then we obeyed the gospel. As soon as we did, all the value of the shed blood of Christ was credited to our account. But the point to notice here is that the sanctification Peter speaks of is a kind that takes place *before* a person is born again.

Positional Sanctification

The moment a person is born again, he becomes positionally sanctified. This means that as far as his standing before God is concerned, he is perfectly set apart to God from the world because he is "in Christ." In a very real sense Christ Himself is his sanctification (1 Cor. 1:30).

Every true believer is a saint; he has been separated to the Lord. This is his *position.* Thus in 1 Corinthians 1:2 all the Christians in the local church in Corinth are described as "sanctified in Christ Jesus, called to be saints." The Corinthian saints weren't always very saintly! They tolerated scandalous sin in the fellowship (1 Cor. 5:1-2). They went to law against one another (1 Cor. 6:1). They had some teachers who denied the Resurrection (1 Cor. 15:12-14). But it was still true of them that as far as their position was concerned, they were saints—sanctified in Christ Jesus.

Now let's look at some of the passages that deal with positional sanctification. In Acts 20:32, the expression "all those who are sanctified" means all believers. In Acts 26:18 the Lord described His people as those "who are sanctified by faith in

Me." The Corinthians are described as having been "washed …sanctified…justified in the name of the Lord Jesus and by the Spirit of our God" (1 Cor. 6:11). And the writer to the Hebrews reminds us that "we have been sanctified through the offering of the body of Jesus Christ once for all" (Heb. 10:10). "For by one offering He hath perfected forever them that are sanctified" (Heb. 10:14, KJV).

Positional sanctification is also indicated at times by the use of the word *holy*. Thus in Colossians 3:12, when Paul addresses the Christians as *holy,* he is referring to their standing before God.

Progressive Sanctification

While there are many scriptures which say that all Christians are sanctified, there are many others which say that they *should* be sanctified. If we fail to distinguish the kinds of sanctification, we can find this very confusing, even apparently contradictory.

Progressive or practical sanctification refers to what we should be in our everyday lives. We should be living lives of separation to God from sin and evil. Saints should be becoming more saintly all the time.

It was this aspect of sanctification that the Lord Jesus referred to in John 17:17, when He prayed for His own, "Sanctify them by Your truth. Your word is truth."

The believer's cooperation is involved in this (2 Tim. 2:21). Wherever you find *exhortations* concerning sanctification or holiness you can be sure that the subject is *practical* sanctification. Thus Paul urged the Corinthians: "…let us cleanse ourselves from all filthiness of the flesh and spirit, perfecting holiness in the fear of God" (2 Cor. 7:1). And in the same vein

Peter wrote, "...as He who called you is holy, you also be holy in all your conduct" (1 Pet. 1:15).

One particular form of practical sanctification concerns separation from immorality:

For this is the will of God, your sanctification: that you should abstain from sexual immorality; that each of you should know how to possess his own vessel in sanctification and honor (1 Thess. 4:3-4).

How does a Christian become more holy, more like the Lord Jesus? The answer is found in 2 Corinthians 3:18:

But we all, with unveiled face, beholding as in a mirror the glory of the Lord, are being transformed into the same image from glory to glory, just as by the Spirit of the Lord.

Practical holiness comes from being occupied with the Lord. It's a principle in life that *we become like what we worship*. The more we meditate on Christ, the more we become like Him. The Holy Spirit works this marvelous transformation—not all at once, but from one degree of glory to another!

Perfect Sanctification

This aspect of sanctification is still future for the believer. When he sees the Savior face-to-face he will be forever set apart from all sin and defilement. He will be morally like the Lord Jesus—perfectly sanctified.

This is what we read about in Colossians 1:22, "...in the body of His flesh through death, to present you holy, and blameless, and above reproach in His sight."

In that day the Church will have its ultimate sanctification: "...that He might present her to Himself a glorious church, not

65

having spot or wrinkle or any such thing, but that she should be holy and without blemish" (Eph. 5:27).

Other passages describe our perfect sanctification without mentioning the word. John, for instance, says: "...we know that when He is revealed, we shall be like Him, for we shall see Him as He is" (1 Jn. 3:2b). And Jude reminds us that our Lord will present us "...faultless before the presence of His glory with exceeding joy" (Jude 24b).

Summary

Now it will be extremely helpful in your study of the Bible to distinguish these various aspects of sanctification. Whenever you find words that deal with holiness, ask yourself, "Is this what happened before conversion? Is this what I am in Christ? Is this what I should be day by day? Or is this what I will be when I am ushered into the glorious presence of our Lord Jesus Christ?"

10
The Indwelling, the Baptism, & the Filling

When we come to study the doctrine of the Holy Spirit, we find there are several important distinctions that must be made. We must see the difference between the *indwelling*, the *baptism*, and the *filling* of the Spirit. We must realize that the baptism of the Spirit is not the same as the baptism with fire. And we must discern between a *sovereign* filling of the Spirit and one which is *our* responsibility.

The Indwelling

As soon as a person is born again, the Holy Spirit of God comes to dwell in his or her body (1 Cor. 6:19): "Or do you not know that your body is the temple of the Holy Spirit who is in you, whom you have from God, and you are not your own?" A person who does not have the Spirit is not really a Christian (Rom. 8:9b). Once the third Person of the Trinity indwells a person, He never leaves (Jn. 14:16). How do we know that He indwells us? We know it immediately because the Word of God *says* so. But as time goes on, we know it by the changes He produces in our lives. The indwelling is not primarily a matter of feelings, although the emotions may be involved. We are never told to pray for the indwelling or to tarry for it. We receive it the moment we believe on the Lord Jesus Christ.

The Baptism of the Spirit

With regard to the *baptism* of the Spirit, the key text is 1 Corinthians 12:13:

For by one Spirit we were all baptized into one body—whether Jews or Gentiles, whether slaves or free—and have all been made to drink into one Spirit.

Here we learn that the baptism is that ministry of the Spirit which places a believer in the Body of Christ, that is, the Church. The initial baptism took place on the Day of Pentecost when the Church was formed. Since then, whenever a person is converted, he or she is added to the Church by the Spirit's baptism.

In other words, all believers have received this baptism without regard to race or culture. It is simultaneous with the new birth, not subsequent to it, and it never needs to be repeated in a Christian's life.

No one is ever *commanded* to be baptized with the Spirit. It happens automatically whenever a sinner receives the Savior. It is not an *emotional* experience. The only way we know it happens is that the Bible tells us.

The Baptism with Fire

The baptism with fire is not the same as the baptism of the Spirit. It is a baptism of *judgment*, not of blessing or privilege.

When John the Baptist was speaking to a mixed audience of believers and unbelievers, he said, "He [Christ] will baptize you with the Holy Spirit and fire" (Mt. 3:11; Lk. 3:16). John then proceeds to explain that the baptism of fire is an act of divine judgment:

His winnowing fan is in His hand, and He will thoroughly clean out His threshing floor, and gather the wheat into His barn; but the chaff He will burn with unquenchable fire (Lk. 3:17; see also Mt. 3:12).

The context explains that fire is *judgment*. It is *not* an enjoyable ecstasy or enthusiasm!

But when there is no mention of unbelievers in his audience, John said, "He will baptize you with the Holy Spirit" (Mk. 1:8; Jn. 1:33). He does not mention fire at all.

The baptism with the Spirit is a *past* event for *believers*. The baptism with fire is a *future* event for *unbelievers*.

Two Aspects of the Filling of the Spirit

The filling of the Spirit is used in two different ways in the New Testament. Unless we see this, we can be quite confused in trying to reconcile the Scriptures on the subject.

First, there is what we might call a "sovereign" filling. For instance, we read that John the Baptist was "filled with the Holy Spirit even from his mother's womb" (Lk. 1:15b). Obviously baby John did not have to meet any conditions in order to be filled! God sovereignly did it in order to prepare the Baptizer for his unique ministry as the forerunner of the Messiah.

There are similar instances of sovereign fillings in the book of Acts. Here are two:

Peter was filled with the Spirit in order to equip him for a fearless address to the Sanhedrin (Acts 4:8-12).

And because the Lord filled Paul with the Spirit, the apostle was enabled to deliver a scathing denunciation of Elymas the Sorcerer (Acts 13:9-11).

Be Filled with the Spirit

The other kind of filling is different. *It is a command* to every believer, not something beyond his or her control. The golden text on the subject is Ephesians 5:18: "And do not be drunk with wine, in which is dissipation, but be filled with the Spirit."

The verb "be filled" here suggests a continuing obligation, not a single crisis experience of the Holy Spirit.[1] It is contrasted to the dissipation of being drunk with wine.[2] Note the following:

Drunk with Wine	Filled with the Spirit
Talk slurred, perhaps incoherent	Talk pure and Christ-exalting
Walk unsteady and staggering	Walk holy and purposeful
Person under the control of alcoholic "spirits"	Person under the control of the Holy Spirit
Loss of control	No loss of self control
Characterized by dissipation	No danger of dissipation
Lowered resistance to sin	Heightened resistance to sin
Disgraceful and shameful	Exemplary and noble
Wine a depressant	The filling a stimulant

How to be Filled

We mentioned before that there are some conditions to be met in order to know the filling of the Spirit. As someone has said, we have to put ourselves "in the way of the blessing." How can a person do this?

Confess and forsake sin without delay (1 Jn. 1:9; Prov. 28:13).
Continually present your body to Christ as a living sacrifice (Rom. 12:1-2).
Fill yourself with the Word of God (Col. 3:16).
Spend much time in worship and prayer (2 Cor. 3:18; Mt. 7:7).
Stay close to Christian fellowship (Heb 10:25).
Do all things to the glory of God (1 Cor. 10:31).

A person who is filled with the Spirit doesn't announce the fact to others. He is self-effacing and Christ-exalting (Jn. 3:30; 16:14). The more he walks in the Spirit, the more he is conscious of his own nothingness and unworthiness.

It's good to remember that the filling of the Spirit is not emotion but holiness. True, the emotions are involved, just as in many other areas of the Christian life, but they are not the main thing. Our human feelings are a *by-product* of the divine filling.

One Final Word

A believer may have what we might call a crisis experience of the Holy Spirit quite distinct from anything we have discussed. This may happen when, for instance, he is restored from backsliding to fellowship with the Lord or when he rededicates himself to Christ in a newer and fuller measure. Such an experience is greatly to be desired, and may involve deep emotions. It is not the same as the indwelling or the baptism. Hopefully it is a crisis that leads to the process we know as the filling, but the filling is not a single attainment. It is a process. To *misname* these ministries of the Spirit with biblical expressions that really describe *other* aspects of the spiritual life only creates doctrinal confusion.

Endnotes

1 In the original there are two tenses used in commands or "imperative" forms. One stresses the act or event (aorist). The one used here (present) frequently stresses continued or repeated action. "Keep being filled" is a possible translation.

2 The KJV rendering, "excess," is a word used today to simply mean "more than your limit." (One could have an excess of cola, coffee, or cake, for example.) *Dissipation* pinpoints continued intemperate living, especially regarding alcohol abuse.

Salvation & Service

When we study God's Word we can save ourselves a lot of error and confusion if we distinguish between passages that deal with *salvation* and those that are concerned with Christian life and *service*.

Salvation Passages

Generally speaking, the salvation passages aren't hard to recognize. They give consistent testimony to the following facts:

As far as God's part is concerned, salvation is *by grace*:

Being justified freely by His grace through the redemption that is in Christ Jesus (Rom. 3:24).

As far as Christ's part is concerned, it is made possible by His substitutionary work on Calvary's Cross:

For He made Him who knew no sin to be sin for us, that we might become the righteousness of God in Him (2 Cor. 5:21).

As far as man is concerned, salvation is by faith, entirely apart from the works of the law:

Knowing that a man is not justified by the works of the law but by faith in Jesus Christ, even we have believed in Christ Jesus, that we might be justified by faith in Christ and not by the works of the law; for by the works of the law no flesh shall be justified (Gal. 2:16).

As far as assurance is concerned, a believer can know he is saved on the authority of the Word of God:

These things I have written to you who believe in the name of the Son of God, that you may know that you have eternal life, and that you may continue to believe in the name of the Son of God (1 Jn. 5:13).

As far as security is concerned, the child of God will never perish or come into eternal judgment for his sins:

27 My sheep hear My voice, and I know them, and they follow Me. 28 And I give them eternal life, and they shall never perish; neither shall anyone snatch them out of My hand. 29 My Father, who has given them to Me, is greater than all; and no one is able to snatch them out of My Father's hand (Jn. 10:27-29).

Service Passages

The difficulty arises when we fail to recognize passages that have to do with Christian life and *service* rather than with salvation. Take John 15:1-11, for example:

1 I am the true vine, and My Father is the vinedresser. 2 Every branch in Me that does not bear fruit He takes away; and every branch that bears fruit He prunes, that it may bear more fruit. 3 You are already clean because of the word which I have spoken to you. 4 Abide in Me, and I in you. As the branch cannot bear fruit of itself, unless it abides in the vine, neither can you, unless you abide in Me. 5 I am the vine, you are the branches. He who abides in Me, and I in him, bears much fruit; for without Me you can do nothing. 6 If anyone does not abide in Me, he is cast out as a branch and is withered; and they gather them and throw them into the fire, and they are burned. 7 If you abide in Me, and My words abide in you, you will ask what you desire, and it shall be done for you. 8 By this My Father is glorified, that you bear much fruit; so you will be My disciples. 9 As the Father loved Me, I also have loved you; abide in My love. 10 If you keep My commandments, you will abide in My love, just as I have kept My Father's commandments and abide in His love. 11 These things I have spoken to you, that My joy may remain in you, and that your joy may be full.

The subject of this paragraph is not salvation from hell, but *fruitbearing*. That is, it concerns the manifestation of the fruit of the Spirit in the life of the Christian (Gal. 5:22-23). It wasn't written to sinners needing a Savior, but to saints needing Christlikeness. If you don't see this, you may come up with the conclusion that Christians may be cast into the fire of hell after all. What John 15:6 actually teaches is that the world takes the name and testimony of a backslidden believer and figuratively throws it into the fire as worthless. Unsaved people have nothing but contempt for a "branch" (a believer) that doesn't abide in the Vine.

Another passage that's often misunderstood is 1 Corinthians 3:10-15:

10 According to the grace of God which was given to me, as a wise master builder I have laid the foundation, and another builds on it. But let each one take heed how he builds on it. 11 *For no other foundation can anyone lay than that which is laid, which is Jesus Christ. 12 Now if anyone builds on this foundation with gold, silver, precious stones, wood, hay, straw, 13 each one's work will become clear; for the Day will declare it, because it will be revealed by fire; and the fire will test each one's work, of what sort it is. 14 If anyone's work which he has built on it endures, he will receive a reward. 15 If anyone's work is burned, he will suffer loss; but he himself will be saved, yet so as through fire.*

The subject of *verse 11* is salvation; it teaches that the Lord Jesus Christ is the only valid foundation. But the rest of the passage deals with building on the foundation—in other words, with *the service that follows salvation.* There's no suggestion that any believer will be tested by fire. It's his *works* that will be tested. The believer himself won't be burned up, but his works may. The emphasis here is not on the faith that leads to salvation but on the works that lead to *reward* or loss of reward.

Or, let's take as another example Paul's words in 1 Corinthians 9:24-27:

24 *Do you not know that those who run in a race all run, but one receives the prize? Run in such a way that you may obtain it. 25 And everyone who competes for the prize is temperate in all things. Now they do it to obtain a perishable crown, but we for an imperishable crown. 26 Therefore I run thus: not with uncertainty. Thus I fight: not as one who beats the air. 27 But I discipline my body and bring it into subjection, lest, when I have preached to others, I myself should become disqualified.*

In the last verse Paul speaks of the possibility of his being "disqualified" (Greek *adokimos*, literally "not approved") in the end. The context does *not* deal with salvation, but with self-control in the Christian life. There was no possibility of Paul's being rejected as to salvation, because he was accepted in Christ. But failure to discipline himself might result in his becoming disqualified as far as service and reward were concerned. (The KJV translation "castaway" in verse 27 is far from literal and has caused much needless grief.)

The distinction between salvation and service is the key to resolving one of the seeming contradictions of the New Testament. In Matthew 12:30 our Lord said:

He who is not with Me is against Me, and he who does not gather with Me scatters abroad.

But in Mark 9:40 the Savior said,

For he who is not against us is on our side.

At first reading these verses seem to be an out-and-out contradiction of each other! But the difficulty disappears when we see that Matthew 12:30 deals with salvation and Mark 9:40 with service. In the first instance, the Lord Jesus was speaking to the Pharisees, who were rejecting Him as the Son of God and accusing Him of performing miracles in the power of the Devil. When it comes to the Person of Christ, anyone who is not for Him is against Him.

The second case was concerned with a man who was serving in the Name of Christ but who was not following the disciples. When they forbade him, Jesus said, "Do not forbid him …for he who is not against us is on our side." When it comes to service for Christ, anyone who is not against us is for us.

These illustrations should show how helpful it is to distinguish passages that deal with salvation from those that deal with Christian life and service. In your Bible study, therefore, ask yourself whether the Scripture you are considering deals with:

- God's work *for* us—salvation
- God's work *in* us—sanctification
- Gods work *through* us—service.

12
Personal Greatness vs. Positional Greatness

There are a few passages of Scripture where it is necessary to discern whether the writer is speaking about a person's *character* or his *role in life*. For instance, a person may be greater than another because he is inherently *better*. On the other hand, superior greatness may only mean that someone holds a higher *office*.

John the Baptist

Jesus said, "Assuredly, I say to you, among those born of women there has not risen one greater than John the Baptist..." (Mt. 11:11a). This does *not* mean that John had a better character than Noah, Daniel, or Job. It doesn't mean that he was more gracious, godly, meek, or loving. What it *does* mean is that his position as forerunner of the Messiah was a role greater than any of his predecessors had ever had. No one else had the privilege of preparing the way of the Lord, of announcing His arrival, and of baptizing Him. In this respect, John was unique.

The Least in the Kingdom

Immediately after speaking of John's *positional* superiority,

Jesus added, "…but he who is least in the kingdom of heaven is greater than he" (Mt. 11:11b). Once again, it does not mean that the least in the kingdom has a better personality or lifestyle than John the Baptist. Rather, the thought is that whereas he announced the kingdom, believers today are *citizens* of the kingdom.[1] John described himself as a "friend of the bridegroom" (Jn. 3:29), whereas God's people today are the *bride*. The bride has a higher position than a friend of the bridegroom and is greater in that regard.

Mary

The angel Gabriel said to the Virgin Mary, "Rejoice, highly favored one, the Lord is with you; blessed are you among women" (Lk. 1:28). There is no question that Mary was a godly young woman, chaste and blameless. But her true greatness consists in the fact that she was chosen to be the mother of our Lord in His humanity. Even she acknowledged herself to be a sinner by calling God her "Savior" (Lk. 1:47). Her character was not *necessarily* greater than Ruth's or Hannah's. But her role was without parallel.

One day an admirer said to Jesus, "Blessed is the womb that bore You, and the breasts which nursed You!" (Lk. 11:27). Jesus replied, "More than that, blessed are those who hear the Word of God and keep it" (v. 28). This means that it is greater to be an obedient follower of Christ even than to be His mother. And it also means that Mary was more blessed by believing on Christ than by giving birth to Him.

The Father is Greater than I

A passage where it is of crucial importance to distinguish between character and position is John 14:28, where Jesus said, "You have heard Me say to you, 'I am going away and coming back to you.' If you loved Me, you would rejoice because I said, 'I am going to the Father,' for My Father is greater than I." The cults and others who deny the Deity of Christ wrench these last words, "My Father is greater than I," completely out of context in an attempt to disprove the equality of the Son with the Father and thus to deny the Trinity.

What, then, does the verse mean? When our Lord spoke these words, He was on earth, enduring all kinds of hostility, reproach, and abuse from His creatures. He was rejected, despised, and humiliated. The Father, on the other hand, was in heaven, completely free from this kind of treatment. In that sense, the Father was greater than the Son—greater in position but not greater in Person. If the disciples really loved the Lord, they would have rejoiced at His announcement that He was returning to heaven, because there He would no longer be subject to human insults and vicious treatment. In heaven His position would be the same as the Father's—immune to His creatures' persecution.

The argument has nothing to do with personal character. In that area, the Son of God is equal in all respects with the Father. But as long as the Son was on earth, enduring hostility from sinners against Himself, the Father was greater than He as to His place or position.

Jesus Greater Than...

In Matthew 12, the Lord Jesus speaks of Himself as greater than the temple (v. 6), greater than Jonah (v. 41), and greater than Solomon (v. 42).[2] Here it is more than a question of position or role. He is greater than the temple in that He designed it and established its ritual. He is greater than Jonah in His Person, His message, and its results. And He is greater than

Solomon in His glory and wisdom; He is the One who put wisdom in that king's mind.

Check the Context

Generally speaking, the context explains whether the subject is *personal character* or *positional dignity*. In any references to the Lord Jesus, there can be no question as to His *personal superiority*! He is always "greater than the greatest and far better than the best."

Endnotes

1 See chapter titled "The Church and the Kingdom."

2 Literally translated, "*something* greater than," probably referring to the kingdom. But since the kingdom's presence was in the Person of the King, it's valid to speak of "*Someone* greater than."

13

Fundamental, Important, or Nonessential Matters

In studying the New Testament, it is essential to distinguish between subjects that are fundamental, those that are important though not necessarily fundamental, and those that are nonessential. While every word of God is inspired, not all passages are given equal emphasis or importance.

When the Lord Jesus was speaking to the Pharisees on one occasion, He said, "...you pay tithe of mint and anise and cumin, and have neglected the weightier matters of the law: justice and mercy and faith" (Mt. 23:23). In other words, He acknowledged that some parts of the law were weightier than others. But He also reminded them that even the less weighty matters of the law required obedience.

So it is that in the Christian faith, there are doctrines that are absolutely fundamental. There are others that are important; some of them are expressly labeled as commandments of the Lord (1 Cor. 14:37). And there are some areas that are left to a believer's own judgment before the Lord.

What Are the Fundamentals?

When we speak of the fundamentals, we are referring to doctrines such as the following:

- The inspiration of the Scriptures. The Bible is the Word of God.

- The trinity. There is one God, existing eternally in three Persons.

- The deity of Christ. The Lord Jesus Christ is God.

- The incarnation. Jesus is also perfect Man.

- His substitutionary death on Calvary, His burial, resurrection, and ascension to heaven.

- The gospel. Salvation by grace, through faith, and apart from works.

- The second advent. Christ is coming again. Though not all agree on the details of His return, the fact itself is a basic tenet of the faith.

- The eternal punishment of the lost.

Now these doctrines are not negotiable. We are to earnestly contend for them. They are clearly taught in the Scriptures. They have been held by the evangelical church down through the centuries. Conflicting views have been labeled heresies. Believers have been willing to die for these precious truths. No compromise is possible. We cannot have fellowship with those who deny the fundamentals.

Of course, this also applies to the unchanging moral laws of God. It's always wrong to commit adultery. It's always sinful to

84

lie and to steal. Idolatry in any form is forbidden by God's Word. In these and many similar areas, there can be no palliating, no ameliorating, no softening. We must stand unequivocally with God against these evils.

Important though not Fundamental

A second class of subjects includes matters that are important because the Bible teaches authoritatively about them. But they have never been considered as fundamentals of the faith. Here are some of the topics that fall under this heading:

- Baptism

- Divorce and remarriage

- The outline of future events

- Election and human responsibility

- The security of the believer

- Women's role in the church

- The gifts of the Spirit

While there is only one right interpretation of each of these subjects, not all believers agree as to what that interpretation is. Great and godly Christians do not see eye to eye. John Wesley would disagree with Charles Spurgeon. In these areas it is incumbent on every one to form convictions based solely and solidly on the Word of God.

Nonessentials or Matters of Moral Indifference

The third classification covers subjects that the Bible treats as nonessentials. These are also called matters of moral indifference. In these areas, the Lord allows for differences of opinion as long as one's behavior does not stumble others (Rom. 14:13), disturb the peace of the church (Rom. 14:19), or violate one's own conscience (Rom. 14:23).

In the early days of the church, problems arose concerning foods that had been offered to idols, the observance of days (the Jewish religious calendar), and foods clean and unclean. The biblical solution can be summarized as follows:

Foods Offered to Idols

With regard to foods that have been offered to idols, the principal passages are 1 Corinthians 8:1-13 and 1 Corinthians 10:14-30. The gist of the teaching there is that it's all right to eat such foods as long as the Christian does not participate in the feast where the food is offered to idols, as long as his conscience is clear in the matter, and as long as he doesn't stumble some other person. But when Paul says, "All things are lawful," we must understand that he is not speaking about all things without exception. He is referring only to the subject at hand—matters of moral indifference. If you don't see this, you might adopt the gross interpretation that Paul would condone immorality!

The Observance of Days

Chapter 14 of Romans deals with the subjects of observance of days, eating meat (in contrast to vegetables only), and drinking wine. Among the other guidelines which Paul lays down is this one: "Let each be fully convinced in his own mind" (v. 5b). Now if you take this out of its context and apply it to such doctrines as the inspiration of the Bible or salvation by grace through faith, you are in serious trouble. It's imperative to see that the principles laid down in Romans 14 deal only with matters that are not black or white in themselves.

Foods Clean and Unclean

In Titus 1, Paul devotes considerable attention to those false teachers who were trying to put the Christian believers under the Law of Moses. In verse 15 the apostle says: "To the pure all things are pure, but to those who are defiled and unbelieving nothing is pure; but even their mind and conscience are defiled."

Now it should be clear that when Paul says, "To the pure all things are pure," he is not stating a universal truth, but he's referring only to such matters as meats that had been condemned as unclean by the Law of Moses. To the Christian in this age of grace, all foods which God has provided for human consumption are pure. The labels "kosher" and "nonkosher," no longer apply.

A statement in Romans 14 that must be understood in this same way is verse 14: "I know and am convinced by the Lord Jesus that there is nothing unclean of itself..." Paul knew as well as we do that certain things are unclean, but here he is only discussing foods like pork, shrimp, or rabbit that were unclean under the Old Testament regime.

Nonessentials Today

While some believers may place considerable importance on some of the following topics, none of them is explicitly emphasized in Scripture. Subjects that might fit into the classification of nonessentials today are:

• Wine versus grape juice at the Lord's Supper

- Unleavened bread versus leavened bread
- Times of meetings
- Use of musical instruments in church meetings
- Use of different reputable Bible versions
- Use of Thee or You in addressing God
- Methods of Christian service

With regard to the last item on the list, that is, methods of Christian service, there is allowance for a certain amount of accommodation to the culture and customs of the people. Thus in 1 Corinthians 9:19-23 Paul tells how he identified with his audiences, without, of course, sacrificing any basic truth or compromising his loyalty to Christ:

> 19 *For though I am free from all men, I have made myself a servant to all, that I might win the more; 20 and to the Jews I became as a Jew, that I might win Jews; to those who are under the law, as under the law, that I might win those who are under the law; 21 to those who are without law, as without law (not being without law toward God, but under law toward Christ), that I might win those who are without law; 22 to the weak I became as weak, that I might win the weak. I have become all things to all men, that I might by all means save some. 23 Now this I do for the gospel's sake, that I may be partaker of it with you.*

But when Paul says, "I have become all things to all men, that I might by all means save some," there's no suggestion that he ever compromised the truth of the gospel or participated in any sinful activity. Where it was possible to make a concession without sacrificing truth (as in the circumcision of Timothy,

Acts 16:3), he made the concession in order to get a greater hearing for his message. But where the truth of salvation by grace apart from law-keeping was at stake (as in the controversy over circumcising Titus, Gal. 2:1-5), Paul never budged an inch.

Conclusion

Let us now summarize the material we have covered.

Concerning fundamentals and the unchanging moral laws of God, there must be absolute agreement and obedience.

Concerning matters that are scripturally important, though not fundamental, each believer should base his judgment and practice as closely on the Word of God as possible.

On nonessentials, there must be latitude for differing opinions, a certain amount of give and take for the sake of unity and peace (Eph. 4:1-6). But even here a Christian must refrain from any form of evil, from stumbling a brother, or from violating his own conscience.

When we are dealing with fundamentals and important matters, certain basic principles apply. But when we are dealing with matters of moral indifference, an entirely different set of rules is applicable. Thus, in speaking of the deity of Christ, Paul would not allow for a difference of opinion by saying, "Let each be fully convinced in his own mind" (Rom. 14:5b). Or if he was dealing with immorality, he would not say, "I know and am convinced by the Lord Jesus that there is nothing unclean of itself" (Rom. 14:14). We must determine if he is speaking about fundamentals, important truths, or peripheral matters.

PART III

DISTINCTIONS IN GOD'S METHODOLOGY

14
Differing Ages

Augustine once said, "Distinguish the ages and the Scriptures harmonize." God has divided all human history into ages: "...by whom also He made the ages" (Heb. 1:2, ASV margin). These ages may be long or short. What distinguishes them is not their length but the way in which God deals with humanity.

Dispensations Defined

While God Himself never changes, His methods do. He works in different ways at different times. We sometimes speak of the way God administers His affairs with man during a particular era as a *dispensation*. Technically, a dispensation does not mean an age but rather an administration, a stewardship, an order, or an economy. But it is difficult for us to think of a dispensation without thinking of time. For example, the history of the United States government has been divided into various administrations. We speak of the Roosevelt administration, the Eisenhower administration, or the Reagan administration. We mean, of course, the manner in which the government was operated while those presidents were in office. The important point is the policies that were followed, but we necessarily link those policies with the particular period of time during which they served.

Dispensations Illustrated

Therefore, in this chapter we will think of a dispensation as the way in which God deals with people during any particular period of history. God's dispensational dealings may be compared to the way in which a home is run. When there are only a husband and wife in the home, a certain program is followed. But when there are several young children, an entirely new set of policies is introduced. As the children mature, the affairs of the home are handled differently again. We see this same pattern in God's dealings with the human race (Gal. 4:1-5).

For example, when Cain killed his brother Abel, God set a mark on him, so that anyone finding him would not put him to death (Gen. 4:15). Yet after the Flood God instituted capital punishment, decreeing that "Whoever sheds man's blood, by man his blood shall be shed" (Gen. 9:6a). Why the difference? Because there had been a change in dispensations.

Another example. In Psalm 137:8-9 the writer calls down severe judgment on Babylon:

8 *O daughter of Babylon, who are to be destroyed, happy the one who repays you as you have served us!*
9 *Happy the one who takes and dashes your little ones against the rock!*

Yet later our Lord taught His people:

...love your enemies, bless those who curse you, do good to those who hate you, and pray for those who spitefully use you and persecute you (Mt. 5:44).

It seems obvious that language suitable for the psalmist living under law would no longer be suitable for a Christian living under grace.

94

Under law, the men of Israel were commanded to put away their heathen wives and children (Ezra 10:3). Under grace, believers should not put away unbelieving mates or children (1 Cor. 7:12-16).

Dispensations Demonstrated

Not all Christians are agreed on the number of dispensations or the names that should be given to them. In fact, some Christians do not accept dispensations at all.

But we may demonstrate the existence of dispensations as follows. First of all, there are at least two dispensations—law and grace: "For the law was given through Moses, but grace and truth came through Jesus Christ" (Jn. 1:17). The fact that our Bibles are divided into Old and New Testaments indicates that a change of administration occurred. Further proof is given by the fact that believers in this age are not required to offer animal sacrifices; this too shows that God has introduced a new order.

But if we agree that there are *two* dispensations, we are forced to believe that there are *three*, because the Dispensation of Law was not introduced until Exodus 19, hundreds of years after Creation. So there must have been at least one dispensation before the Law (see Rom. 5:14). That makes three.

And then we should be able to agree on a *fourth* dispensation, because the Scriptures speak of "the age to come" (Heb. 6:5). This is the time when the Lord Jesus Christ will return to reign over the earth, otherwise known as the Millennium. (*Millennium* is Latin for one thousand years.)

The apostle Paul also distinguishes between the present age and an age to come. First he speaks of a dispensation that was committed to him in connection with the truth of the gospel and the Church (1 Cor. 9:17; Eph. 3:2; Col. 1:25). That is the present age. But then he also points forward to a future age when, in Ephesians 1:10, he refers to "the dispensation of the fullness of the times." It is apparent from his description of it that it has not yet arrived.

So we know that we are not living in the final age of the world's history.

Dispensations Specified

Dr. C. I. Scofield, editor of the Scofield Reference Bible lists seven dispensations, as follows:

1. Innocence (Gen. 1:28). From Adam's creation to his fall.
2. Conscience or Moral Responsibility (Gen. 3:7, 22). From the fall to the end of the Flood.
3. Human Government (Gen. 9:5-6). From the end of the Flood to the call of Abraham.
4. Promise (Gen. 12:1-3). From the call of Abraham to the giving of the Law.
5. Law (Ex. 19–20). From the giving of the Law to the Day of Pentecost.
6. Church (Acts 2). From the Day of Pentecost to the Rapture.
7. Kingdom (Rev. 20:4). The thousand-year reign of Christ.

In his chart, "The Course of Time from Eternity to Eternity," A. E. Booth sees seven dispensations of human history foreshadowed in the seven days of Genesis:

- First day—Man tested with the light of creation light and promise.
- Second day—Government (from the Flood to the dividing of the nations).
- Third day—Israel (from Abraham to the end of the Gospels).
- Fourth day—Grace (a parenthetic period).
- Fifth day—The Tribulation.
- Sixth day—The Millennium.
- Seventh day—Eternity.

Importance of Dispensations

While it's not important to agree on the exact details, it is quite important to see that different dispensations do exist. (The distinction between law and grace is especially important.) Otherwise we will take portions of Scripture that apply to other ages and refer them to ourselves. While all Scriptures are profitable for us (2 Tim. 3:16), not all were written *directly to us*. Passages dealing with other ages have applications for us, but their primary interpretation is for the age for which they were written. For example, Jews living under the Law were forbidden to eat the meat of any unclean animal, that is, one that did not have a cloven hoof and did not chew the cud (Lev. 11:3). This prohibition is not binding on Christians today (Mk. 7:18-19), but the underlying principle remains that we should avoid moral and spiritual uncleanness.

God promised the people of Israel that if they obeyed Him, He would make them materially prosperous (Deut. 28:1-6).

The emphasis then was on material blessings in earthly places. But this is not true today. God does not promise that He will reward our obedience with *financial* prosperity. Instead, the blessings of this dispensation are *spiritual* blessings in the heavenly places (Eph. 1:3).

One Gospel for All Dispensations

While there are differences among the various ages, there is one thing that never changes, and that is the gospel. Salvation always has been, is now, and always will be by faith in the Lord. And the basis of salvation for every age is the finished work of Christ on Calvary's Cross. People in the Old Testament were saved by believing whatever revelation the Lord gave them. Abraham, for example, was saved by believing God when He said that the patriarch's seed would be as numerous as the stars (Gen. 15:5-6). So far as we can determine, Abraham did not know much, if anything, about what would take place at Calvary centuries later. But God knew. And when Abraham believed the Lord, He put to Abraham's account all the value of the future work of Christ at Calvary.

Someone has said that the Old Testament saints were saved "on credit." That is to say, they were saved on the basis of the price that the Lord Jesus would pay many years later (that is the meaning of Rom. 3:25). We are saved on the basis of the work which Christ accomplished over 1900 years ago. But in both cases salvation is by faith in the Lord.

We must guard against any idea that people in the Dispensation of Law were saved by keeping the Law or even by offering animal sacrifices. The Law can only condemn; it cannot save (Rom. 3:20). And the blood of bulls and goats cannot put away a single sin (Heb. 10:4). No! God's way of salvation is by faith and faith alone! (See Rom. 5:1.)

Another good point to remember is this: when we speak of the present age as being the Age of Grace, we do not imply that God was not gracious in past dispensations. We simply mean that God is now *testing* man under grace rather than under law. This distinction will be explained more fully in a future chapter.

It is also important to realize that the ages do not close with split-second precision. Often there is an overlapping or transition period. We see this in the Book of Acts, for instance; it took some time for the new Church to throw off some of the trappings of the previous dispensation. And it's possible that there will be a period of time between the Rapture and the Tribulation during which the Man of Sin will be manifested and the Temple will be erected in Jerusalem.

Abuse of Dispensations

One final word. Like all good things, the study of dispensations can be abused. There are some Christians who carry dispensationalism to such an extreme that they accept only Paul's Prison Epistles as applicable for the Church today! As a result they do not accept baptism or the Lord's Supper, since these are not found in the Prison Epistles. They also teach that Peter's gospel message was not the same as Paul's. (See Gal. 1:8-9 for a refutation of this.) These people are sometimes called ultra-dispensationalists or Bullingerites (after a teacher named E. W. Bullinger). Their extreme view of dispensations should be rejected.

15
Major Covenants of Scripture

At various intervals in human history, God made agreements or covenants with mankind. Some of them, like the Law, were *conditional*. God would keep His part of the covenant if they kept theirs. Conditional covenants were "weak through the flesh," and man invariably failed to meet the conditions.

Fortunately, most of the divine covenants were *unconditional*. In them, everything depends on the Lord, and that guarantees their fulfillment.

Most of the covenants were made with Abraham and his descendants. None was directly made with the Church, although the Church is involved in a few, as we shall see.

Eden (Gen. 1:28-30; 2:16-17)

The Edenic Covenant made man, in his innocence, responsible to multiply, populate the earth, and subdue it. He was given authority over all animal life. He was to cultivate the garden and eat of all its produce, except the fruit of the tree of knowledge of good and evil. Disobedience to this latter command would bring death. Therefore it was a conditional covenant.

Adam (Gen. 3:14-19)

After the fall of man, God cursed the serpent and predicted

enmity between the serpent and the woman, and between Satan and Christ. Satan would injure Christ, but Christ would destroy Satan. Woman would experience pain in childbirth and would be under the authority of her husband. The ground was cursed: man would have to contend with thorns and thistles in cultivating it. This would involve sweat and weariness, and his body would eventually return to dust, from which it came.

Noah (Gen. 8:20–9:27)

God promised Noah that He would not curse the ground again or destroy the earth with a flood, giving the rainbow as a pledge. The covenant decrees capital punishment for the crime of murder, and this, of course, assumes that there will be a government to try the case and to execute the penalty. So in a real sense, the Noahic covenant establishes human government. God guaranteed the regularity of time periods and the seasons, directed man to repopulate the earth, and reaffirmed his dominion over lower creatures. Man could now add meat to his previously vegetarian diet. Concerning Noah's descendants, God cursed Ham's son, Canaan,[1] to be a servant to Shem and Japheth. He gave Shem a place of favor, which we know includes being in the line of the Messiah. Japheth would enjoy great expansion, and would dwell in the tents of Shem. The covenant with Noah was unconditional and has never been revoked. It was for "perpetual generations" (Gen. 9:12).

Abraham (Gen. 12:1-3; 13:14-17; 15:1-5; 17:1-8)

This covenant includes the following unconditional promises to Abram, later called Abraham, and his descendants: A great nation (Israel); personal blessing to Abraham; a name of renown; a source of blessing to others (12:2). Divine favor to

102

his friends and a curse on his enemies; blessing to all nations (fulfilled through Christ) (12:3). Everlasting possession of the land known as Canaan and later as Israel and Palestine (15:18). Numerous posterity, natural and spiritual (13:16; 15:5). A father of many nations and kings (through Ishmael and Isaac) (17:4, 6). A special relationship to God (17:7b).

The Law, also called the Mosaic Covenant (Ex. 19:5; 20–31)

In its broadest sense, the Mosaic law includes the Ten Commandments, describing duties to God and to one's neighbor (Ex. 20); numerous regulations concerning the social life of Israel (Ex. 21:1–24:11); and detailed ordinances dealing with religious life (Ex. 24:12–31:18). It was given to the nation of Israel, not to the Gentiles, and confirmed in blood (Ex. 24:8; Heb. 9:19-20). It was a conditional covenant, requiring man's obedience, and therefore it was "weak through the flesh" (Rom. 8:3a). The Decalogue was never intended to provide salvation, but rather to produce conviction of sin and failure (Rom. 3:20b). Nine of the Ten Commandments are repeated in the New Testament (the Sabbath excepted), *not* as law with *penalty* attached, but as behavior suitable for those who have been saved by grace. The Christian is under grace, not law, but he is "enlawed" to Christ (1 Cor. 9:21), a far higher constraint. The law did not annul the Abrahamic Covenant (Gal. 3:17-18).

Palestine (Deut. 28:1; 29:1-30:20).

This covenant was found in seed-form in Genesis 15:18, when God promised Abraham the land "from the river of Egypt [the Brook of Egypt, not the Nile] to the great river, the River Euphrates." It foresees the dispersion of Israel among the nations because of disobedience and unfaithfulness, their return to the Lord at His Second Advent, their repentance and conversion, the punishment of their enemies, and their dwelling securely in the land under the reign of the Messiah.

Israel has never fully occupied the land. During Solomon's reign, countries in the eastern portion paid *tribute* (1 Ki. 4:21, 24), but that cannot be counted as possession or occupation. The fulfillment of the Palestinian Covenant is still future.

David (2 Sam. 7:1-17)

God promised David not only that his kingdom would endure forever, but that he would also have descendants to sit upon the throne (2 Sam. 7:12-16). It was an unconditional covenant, not dependent in any way on David's obedience or righteousness. Christ is the *legal* heir to the throne of David through Solomon, as is seen in Joseph's genealogy in Matthew 1. Joseph adopted Jesus as his son. Christ is a *lineal* descendant of David through Nathan, as is seen in Mary's genealogy in Luke 3. Because he lives forever, there can be no other claimant to the throne. His kingdom is everlasting. His 1,000 year reign will merge into the eternal kingdom.

Solomon (2 Sam. 7:12-15; 1 Ki. 9; 2 Chron. 7)

The covenant with Solomon was unconditional as far as the everlasting kingdom was concerned, but conditional as far as his descendants sitting on the throne (1 Ki. 9:4-5; 2 Chron. 7:17-18). One of Solomon's descendants, Coniah (also called Jeconiah and Jehoiachin), was barred from having any physical descendant sit upon David's throne (Jer. 22:30). Jesus is not a descendant of Solomon, as pointed out above. Otherwise he would have come under the curse of Coniah.

The New Covenant (Jer. 31:31-34; Heb. 8:7-12; Lk. 22:20)

The new covenant is clearly made with the house of Israel and the house of Judah (Jer. 31:31) and it supersedes the Old (Mosaic) Covenant. It has a better priesthood, a better High Priest, a better sacrifice, a better altar, and rests on better promises (Heb. 7–9; 13:10). It was still future when Jeremiah wrote (Jer. 31:31a). It is not a conditional covenant, like the Mosaic law, which Israel broke (Jer. 31:32). In it God uncon-ditionally promises (note the repetition of "I will"): Israel's future regeneration (Ezek. 36:25-26); the indwelling of the Holy Spirit (Ezek. 36:27); a heart that is favorably disposed to do the will of God (Jer. 31:33a); universal knowledge of the law in Israel (Jer. 31:34a); forgiveness and oblivion of sins (Jer. 31:34b); and the continuance of the nation forever (Jer. 31:35-37).

Israel as a nation has not as yet received the benefits of the new covenant, but will at the Lord's second advent. In the meantime, true believers do share some of the blessings of the covenant. They enjoy the forgiveness and oblivion of sins (Heb. 10:16-17) and are enabled to fulfill the righteous requirement of the law (Rom. 8:4). The fact that the Church is related to the new covenant is seen in the Lord's Supper, where the cup represents the covenant and the blood by which it was ratified (Lk. 22:20; 1 Cor. 11:25).[2] Also Paul spoke of himself and the other apostles as "ministers of a new covenant" (2 Cor. 3:6), meaning the gospel of the grace of God.

Endnotes

1 A curse generally reverted to the father of the person who received it, showing his responsibility for raising his son. Arthur Custance writes: "…Noah could not pronounce judgment of any kind upon his own son, Ham, the actual offender, without passing judgment upon himself, for society held him, the father, responsible for his son's behavior" (*Noah's Three Sons*, p. 195). A. W. Pink notes: "Ham's sin consisted of an utter failure to *honor his father*….And mark the fearful consequence: he reaped exactly as he had sown—Ham sinned as a *son* and was punished *in his son*" (*Gleanings in Genesis*, p. 124, author's italics).

2 J. N. Darby pointed out that the Church personally knows the *Mediator* of the New Covenant, which is better than being the primary subject of it.

16
Israel, the Gentiles & the Church

The New Testament divides all mankind into three categories: Israel, the Gentiles, and the Church. For example, Paul says in 1 Corinthians 10:32, "Give no offense, either to the Jews or to the Greeks or to the church of God." Here the word "Greeks" is synonymous with "Gentiles."

In Acts 15:14-17 these three sections of humanity are mentioned again:

The Church

..."God at the first did visit the Gentiles to take out of them ***a people for His name"*** (v. 14, emphasis added).

Israel

"After this I will return and will rebuild ***the tabernacle of David****, which has fallen down; I will rebuild its ruins, and I will set it up"* (v. 16, emphasis added).

The Gentile Nations

"So that the rest of mankind may seek the Lord, even ***all the Gentiles*** *who are called by My name, says the Lord who does all these things"* (v. 17, emphasis added).

The Apostle Paul also distinguished between:

- the Jews—the circumcision made with hands (Eph. 2:11).
- the Gentiles—the uncircumcision (Eph. 2:11).
- the Church—the circumcision made without hands (Col. 2:11).

Generally speaking, Bible students do not confuse the Gentiles with either Israel or the Church; that has not been a problem. So in this lesson we will confine ourselves to the distinction between Israel and the Church. This is of great importance. Unless we see that these two groups are separate and distinct, it will seriously affect our interpretation of the Bible, especially in the areas of Church truth and prophecy.

In order to show why the subject is important, we should mention that some people teach that the Church is merely an extension or an outgrowth of Israel. They say, "God has had a continuing Church down through the centuries. Israel was the Church in the Old Testament, but when that people rejected the Messiah, God rejected them forever. There is no future for Israel nationally. The New Testament Church has now become the Israel of God, and all the promises made to Israel nationally now have a spiritual fulfillment for the Church."

We believe that the Scriptures teach otherwise—that Israel and the Church are different in origin, character, responsibility, and destiny.

When Israel rejected the Lord Jesus as her Messiah, God set the nation aside for a time. Then He introduced something entirely new—the Church. When His program with the Church is finished on earth, He will resume His dealings with Israel nationally. So the Church has been brought in as a sort of parenthesis during the interruption of God's relations with Israel, His ancient people.

The distinction between the Church and Israel may best be seen by the following set of contrasts.

The Church	Israel
1. Paul speaks of the Church as a mystery "which in other ages was not made known to the sons of men, as it has now been revealed by the Spirit to His holy apostles and prophets" (Eph. 3:5). He says that this mystery was hidden in God from the beginning of the world (Eph. 3:9) and kept secret since the world began, but that it is now made manifest by the prophetic Scriptures (Rom. 16:25-26). (See also Col. 1:25-26.)	1. Israel is never spoken of as a mystery. None of the descriptions in the opposite column are true of Israel.
2. The Church began at Pentecost when the Holy Spirit was given (Acts 2). We deduce this from the following series of facts:	2. The nation of Israel began with the call of Abraham (Gen. 12).
a. The Church was still future when Christ was on earth, because He said, "I *will* build [future tense] My church" (Mt. 16:18).	
b. When Paul wrote his first letter to the congregation in Corinth, obviously the Church had by then come into being. He speaks of the believers having been baptized by the Spirit into the body of Christ (1 Cor. 12:13).	
c. We know that the promised baptism of the Spirit took place at Pentecost. Therefore, that was the birthday of the Church.	

109

The Church	Israel
3. Christ is the Head of the Church.	3. Abraham was the head of Israel.
4. Membership in the Church is by spiritual birth.	4. Membership in the nation was by natural birth.
5. The Church is God's heavenly people. The blessings of the Church are spiritual blessings in heavenly places.	5. Israel was God's chosen earthly people. The blessings of Israel were primarily, though not exclusively, material blessings in earthly places.
The citizenship of Christians is heavenly.	The citizenship of Israelites was earthly.
The hope of the Church is to be with Christ in heaven.	The primary hope held before Israel was the earthly reign of Messiah in the land (This does not deny that believing Israelites went to heaven when they died, or that they had the hope of heaven. But that was not the emphasis that was set before them.)
6. In the Church, believing Jews and believing Gentiles become one new man in Christ. They become fellow-heirs, fellow-members of the body, and fellow-partakers of the promise in Christ by the gospel. In Christ, the middle wall of partition between Jew and Gentile is broken down, and both are made one (Eph. 2:13-17; Eph. 3:6).	6. None of this is true of Israel. As far as Israel is concerned, Gentiles are "without Christ, being aliens from the commonwealth of Israel and strangers from the covenants of promise, having no hope and without God in the world" (Eph. 2:12).

The Church	Israel
7. In the Church, all believers are priests—holy priests and royal priests. As such they have access to the presence of God by faith at any time (1 Pet. 2:1-9; Heb. 10:19-22).	7. In Israel, the priests were chosen from the tribe of Levi and the family of Aaron. Only the high priest could enter the presence of God, and only on one day of the year (Heb. 7:5, 11; 9:7)
8. The Church will be taken home to heaven at the Rapture, then will return with Christ and reign with Him over the earth during the Millennium.	8. Redeemed Israel will be the earthly subjects of Christ when He reigns.

Many more contrasts between the Church and Israel could be listed. In the fourth volume of his *Systematic Theology* (pp. 47-53), Lewis Sperry Chafer enumerates twenty-four unmistakable distinctions. But the ones we have given should be sufficient to show that the Church occupies a unique place in the plans and purposes of God, and that it must not be confused with Israel.

One of the Scripture passages in which Israel and the Church are regularly confused is the Olivet Discourse, found in Matthew 23:37–25:46. This passage concerns Israel—not the Church. It describes conditions prior to and including the return of Christ to reign as King. Notice that it says in 24:16, "Then let those who are in *Judea* flee to the mountains"—the locale is clearly Jewish. And in verse 20 we read, "And pray that your flight may not be...on the Sabbath." The Sabbath was never given to the Church—only to Israel. The elect mentioned in verse 22 are God's *Jewish* elect. The coming of Christ described in verse 30 is not His coming into the air for the Church, but His coming to the earth as Israel's King.

So the Bible student should discern whether a passage is referring to Israel or to the Church. If you are reading about the Day of the Lord, you can be sure that the passage refers primarily to Israel. If, on the other hand, you come to references to the Day of Christ, you can be sure the Church is in view. Thus the seventh trumpet of Revelation 11 has to do with Israel, because that is part of the Day of the Lord. But the "last trumpet" of 1 Corinthians 15:52 relates to the Church, because the subject is the Rapture, and the Rapture is connected with the Day of Christ.

In closing, we must consider two of the arguments most commonly used to attempt to prove that the Church is *not* distinct from Israel.

1. In Acts 7:38 (KJV), Israel is called "the church in the wilderness." But we must realize that the word translated "church" (*ekklesia*) simply means an assembly or company of people. The NKJV rendering "congregation," a word still favored in Jewish circles today, better captures this truth. The same word is used to describe a heathen mob in Ephesus (Acts 19:32). The New Testament Church is identified as being related to God the Father and the Lord Jesus Christ.

2. In Galatians 6:16, Paul says, "And as many as walk according to this rule, peace and mercy be upon them, and upon the Israel of God." The expression "the Israel of God" is used to assert that all believers today constitute "the Israel of God." But we believe this is a misunderstanding. When Paul says, "Peace be on them," he is referring to all believers. But in the words "the Israel of God" Paul singles out those believers of Jewish birth who walk according to the rule of the new

creation (v. 15) and not according to the rule of the law. (The NIV's rendering here of the usual Greek word for "and" *(kai)* as "*even* the Israel of God," while not grammatically impossible, shows the amillennial bias of some of its key editors. This unfortunate translation tends to rob Israel of all her promises and make the Church "the new Israel.")

17
Law & Grace

Law and grace are two opposite ways in which God deals with the human race. We can describe them as dissimilar principles under which He tests man. Or we may think of them as two covenants that He has made with His people: "For the law was given through Moses, but grace and truth came through Jesus Christ" (Jn. 1:17).

Under the principle of law, a person receives what he earns or deserves. Under grace he is spared from what he deserves and is enriched beyond description—all as a free gift. The two principles are described in Romans 4:4-5:

> 4 *Now to him who works, the wages are not counted as grace but as debt. 5 But to him who does not work but believes on Him who justifies the ungodly, his faith is accounted for righteousness.*

Grace and law are mutually exclusive; that is, they cannot be mixed. "And if by grace, then it is no longer of works; otherwise grace is no longer grace" (Rom. 11:6a).

Law is a *conditional* covenant: God says, "If you obey, I will reward you, but if you disobey, I must punish you." Grace is an *unconditional* covenant: God says, "I will bless you freely."

The law says, *"Do,"* whereas grace says, *"Believe."* But believing is *not* a condition; it's the only reasonable response of a creature to his or her Creator. And it's not meritorious; no

115

one can be proud that he has believed on the Lord. He would be stupid not to believe on the only totally dependable Person in the universe.

Under law, holiness is required but no power is given to live a holy life. Under grace holiness is taught (Titus 2:11-12) and the necessary power is given. Someone has put it this way: "The law demands strength from one who has none and curses him if he can't display it. Grace gives strength to one who has none and blesses him in the exhibition of it."

The law brings a curse: "Cursed is everyone who does not continue in all things which are written in the book of the law, to do them" (Gal. 3:10b). Grace brings a blessing: "Being justified freely by His grace through the redemption that is in Christ Jesus" (Rom. 3:24).

Under law bragging is encouraged, but under grace it is ruled out. "Then what becomes of our boasting? It is excluded. On what principle? On the principle of works? No, but on the principle of faith" (Rom. 3:27, RSV).

There can't be any assurance of salvation under law; you could never know whether you had performed enough good works—or the right kind of good works. Under grace there is full assurance because salvation is a gift; you *know* when you have received a gift!

A person under law could not have true security because he could not be sure he would *continue* to meet the requirements. Under grace the believer enjoys eternal security (Jn. 10:27-29) because his salvation depends on the perfect work of Christ.

There is no salvation by the law. God never intended that anyone would ever be saved on that principle. The purpose of the law is to show a person that he's a sinner. "By the law is the knowledge of sin" (Rom. 3:20b)—not the knowledge of salvation.

Salvation is by grace (Eph. 2:8-9). It's the free, undeserved gift of God to those who receive the Lord Jesus Christ as their only hope for heaven.

Under law sin is *aroused* (Rom. 7:8-13); under grace sin is *despised*. When sinful man is put under law he immediately wants to do what's forbidden. It's not the law's fault, but the response of sin in man's nature. Under grace, sin is despised. The memory of what our sins cost the Savior makes us turn away from them.

Under law the work is never finished. That's why the Sabbath, the seventh day, came at the *end* of a week of toil. Grace tells us of a finished work, so we *begin* our week with the Lord's Day, our day of rest.

The law tells what man must do. Grace reveals what God has already done in Christ.

The law is a system of bondage (Gal. 4:1-3); grace is a system of liberty (Gal. 5:1). People under law are *servants;* people under grace are *sons* and *daughters.*

The law says, "You shall love..." But grace says, "God so loved ..."

The law says, "Do and you shall live." Grace says, "Live and you will do."

The law says, "Try and obey." Grace says, "Trust and obey."

The law makes demands. Grace bestows favors.

The law condemns the best. Grace justifies the worst.

The law is something to be kept. Grace is something that keeps.

The law leaves a person without excuse. Grace provides an Advocate.

Under law a wayward son was taken outside the city and stoned to death (Deut. 21:18-21). Under grace the prodigal son can confess his sin and come back into the fellowship of his father's house again (Lk. 15:21-24).

Under law the sheep die for the shepherd. Under grace the Shepherd dies for the sheep (Jn. 10:11).

The superiority of grace has been described as follows: Grace is not looking for good people whom it may approve, because it is not grace but justice to approve goodness; but it is looking for condemned, guilty, speechless, and helpless people whom it may save, sanctify, and glorify.

Martin Luther said that if you can rightly distinguish between law and grace, you should thank God for your skill and consider yourself to be an able theologian.

18
The Church &
the Kingdom

It will probably come as a surprise to many readers to learn that the Church is not the same as the kingdom of God or the kingdom of heaven. In Christendom at large the Church and the kingdom are usually taken as synonymous. But failure to distinguish them leads to serious problems in both doctrine and practice.

In chapter sixteen we discussed the Church at some length, so it's not necessary to go over that material again. It's enough to remind ourselves that the Church is a unique society, unlike any other in God's dealings with humanity. Christ is the Head, and all believers are members. Distinctions of race, social status, and sex are abolished in Christ; all become one in Him. The Church began at Pentecost and will be completed at the Rapture. It is spoken of as the body and bride of Christ, and is destined to reign with Him in His Kingdom and to share His glory eternally.

But what about the kingdom of heaven?

The kingdom of heaven is the sphere in which God's rule is acknowledged. The word *heaven* is used figuratively to denote God; this is clearly shown in Daniel 4:25-26. In verse 25, Daniel said that the Most High rules in the kingdom of men. In the very next verse he says that Heaven rules. Thus the kingdom of heaven announces the rule of God, which exists wherever people submit to that rule.

There are two aspects of the kingdom of heaven. The broadest aspect includes everyone who merely professes to acknowledge God as the Supreme Ruler. But its *inner aspect* includes only people who have been genuinely *converted*. We may picture this by two concentric circles, a small one inside a large one.

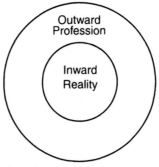

The large circle is the sphere of profession; it includes the true and the false, the wheat and the tares. The inner circle includes only those who have been born again through faith in the Lord Jesus Christ.

By a comparison of all the biblical references to the kingdom, we can trace its historical development in five distinct phases.

The Kingdom Predicted

First of all, the kingdom was *prophesied* in the Old Testament. Daniel predicted that God would set up a kingdom that would never be destroyed and never would yield its sovereignty to another people (Dan. 2:44). He also foresaw the coming of Christ and His universal and everlasting dominion (Dan. 7:13-14; see also Jer. 23:5-6).

The Kingdom at Hand

Second, the kingdom was described as being *at hand* and *present* in the Person of the King. First, John the Baptist, then Jesus, then the disciples announced that the kingdom was at hand (Mt. 3:2; 4:17; 10:7). The King had arrived to present Himself to the nation of Israel. Jesus said, "...if I cast out demons by the Spirit of God, surely the kingdom of God has come upon you" (Mt. 12:28). On another occasion He said, "...the kingdom of God is in the midst of you" (Lk. 17:21, RSV). It was present because the King had arrived on the scene. (While the last two references deal with the kingdom of God rather than the kingdom of heaven, we shall demonstrate below that the two terms are used interchangeably in the New Testament.)

The Interim Kingdom

Third, the kingdom is described in an interim form. After He was rejected by the nation of Israel, the King returned to heaven. The kingdom exists today in the hearts of all who acknowledge His kingship while the King is absent, and the moral and ethical principles of the kingdom are applicable to us today. This interim phase of the kingdom is described in the parables of Matthew 13.

The Kingdom Manifested

The fourth phase of the kingdom is its *manifestation*. This is the literal, thousand-year reign of Christ on earth, often called the Millennium. It was foreshadowed on the Mount of

121

Transfiguration, when the Lord was seen in the glory of His coming reign (Mt. 16:28). Jesus referred to this kingdom when He said, "Many will come from east and west, and sit down with Abraham, Isaac, and Jacob in the kingdom of heaven" (Mt. 8:11).

The Eternal Kingdom

The fifth and final form will be the *everlasting* kingdom. It is described in 2 Peter 1:11 as "the everlasting kingdom of our Lord and Savior Jesus Christ."

The Kingdom of Heaven and the Kingdom of God

The phrase "kingdom of heaven" is found only in Matthew's Gospel. The term "kingdom of God" is found in all four Gospels. For all practical purposes there is no difference; the same things are said about both. For example, in Matthew 19:23 Jesus said it would be hard for a rich man to enter the kingdom of *heaven*. In Mark 10:23 and Luke 18:24 Jesus is quoted as saying the same thing with regard to the kingdom of *God*. In the same Matthew passage Jesus is then quoted as saying virtually the same thing with regard to the kingdom of God (compare Mt. 19:23 and 19:24).

Other passages in which the kingdom of heaven and the kingdom of God are used interchangeably are:

Compare Matthew 4:17 with Mark 1:15
Compare Matthew 8:11 with Luke 13:29
Compare Matthew 10:7 with Luke 9:2
Compare Matthew 11:11 with Luke 7:28
Compare Matthew 13:11 with Mark 4:11
Compare Matthew 13:31 with Mark 4:30-31; Luke 13:18

Compare Matthew 13:33 with Luke 13:20-21
Compare Matthew 19:14 with Mark 10:14; Luke 18:16

We mentioned that the kingdom of heaven has an outward aspect and an inner reality. The same is true of the kingdom of God. This can be demonstrated as follows:

Kingdom of Heaven	Kingdom of God
In its outward aspect it includes all who are genuine subjects of the King, and also those who merely profess allegiance to Him. This is seen in the parable of the sower (Mt. 13:3-11), the parable of the grain of mustard seed (Mt. 13:31, 32), and the parable of the leaven (Mt. 13:33).	It too includes the real and the false. This is seen in the parable of the sower (Lk. 8:4-10), the parable of the grain of mustard seed (Lk. 13:18-19), and the parable of the leaven (Lk. 13:20-21).
As to its true, inward reality, the kingdom of heaven can be entered only by those who are converted (Mt. 18:3).	As to its true, inward reality, the kingdom of God can be entered only by those who are born again (Jn. 3:3, 5).

The apostle Paul was referring to its inward reality when he said that "the kingdom of God is not eating and drinking, but righteousness and peace and joy in the Holy Spirit" (Rom. 14:17). He also emphasized that "the kingdom of God is not in word but in power" (1 Cor. 4:20).

The Kingdom and the Church

The distinction between the kingdom and the Church may be seen in the following: The kingdom began when Christ initiated His public ministry; the Church began on the Day of Pentecost (Acts 2). The kingdom will continue on earth till the earth is destroyed; the Church will continue on earth only until the Rapture; later it will return with Christ at His Second Advent to reign with Him as His bride. *At the present time* the people who are in the kingdom in its true, inner reality are also in the Church; *this is the only respect in which the two overlap.*

Part IV

DISTINCTIONS IN FUTURE EVENTS

19
The Two Comings of Christ

To understand and enjoy the Scriptures, it is necessary to differentiate between the first and second comings of Christ. His First Coming refers, of course, to His birth as a baby in Bethlehem's manger. The Second Coming points forward to the time when He will return. The first is concerned with the sufferings of Christ, the second with the glory that will follow (1 Pet. 1:11).

In this chapter we will present Christ's Second Coming in a general way, presenting only the simple fact that the Savior is coming again. In the next chapter we will see that there are several phases to His Second Coming.

The Old Testament prophets foresaw the coming of the Messiah, but they were confused by what they saw. The Spirit of God revealed to them that the Christ (the Greek word for *Messiah*) would come in both humiliation and glory. He would suffer, bleed, and die, but He would also triumph over all His foes. They could not reconcile this. What they didn't realize was that they were dealing with two distinct advents of the Messiah, with more than 2000 years between them.

The two comings are often merged together in the Bible with no indication of an intervening time period. If we can learn to detect these quick transitions, it will add greatly to our pleasure and profit. Here are some examples.

Examples of Texts about Both Advents

The first twenty-one verses of Psalm 22 clearly refer to the First Advent; they depict the sufferings of the Savior on the Cross. But there is a distinct break between verses 21 and 22. The last ten verses of the psalm point forward to the victory and glory of the Second Advent.

We also find the two comings in Isaiah 9:6-7:

6 For unto us a Child is born, unto us a Son is given; and the government will be upon His shoulder. And His name will be called Wonderful, Counselor, Mighty God, 7 Everlasting Father, Prince of Peace. Of the increase of His government and peace there will be no end, upon the throne of David and over His kingdom, to order it and establish it with judgment and justice from that time forward, even forever. The zeal of the Lord of hosts will perform this.

The coming to Bethlehem is described by the words "For unto us a Child is born, unto us a Son is given . . ." All the rest of the verses point forward to the time when He will return to reign in power and great glory.

The two advents are also found in Isaiah 49:7:

Thus says the Lord, the Redeemer of Israel, their Holy One, to Him whom man despises, to Him whom the nation abhors, to the Servant of rulers: "Kings shall see and arise, princes also shall worship, because of the Lord who is faithful, the Holy One of Israel, and He has chosen You."

The first advent is apparent in the words "to Him whom man despises, to Him whom the nation abhors, to the Servant of rulers," but the rest of the verse points unmistakably to His second coming.

Now notice Isaiah 52:14-15:

14 Just as many were astonished at you, so His visage was marred more than any man, and His form more than the sons of men; 15 so shall He sprinkle many nations. Kings shall shut their mouths at Him; for what had not been told them they shall see, and what they had not heard they shall consider.

Verse 14 obviously describes the Savior on the Cross; those who watched the Crucifixion were astonished at the depths of His suffering. He was so disfigured that He was no longer recognizable as a man. But there is a tremendous contrast in verse 15. When the Savior comes back, men will be astonished at the brilliance of His glory. The nations will be startled to see the lowly Stranger of Galilee returning as King of kings and Lord of lords.

One of the best-known examples of a passage where the two advents are blended is Isaiah 61:1-2:

1 The Spirit of the Lord God is upon Me, because the Lord has anointed Me to preach good tidings to the poor; he has sent Me to heal the brokenhearted, to proclaim liberty to the captives, and the opening of the prison to those who are bound; 2 to proclaim the acceptable year of the Lord, and the day of vengeance of our God; to comfort all who mourn.

When Jesus was in the synagogue in Nazareth He quoted from these verses (Lk. 4:18-19). But notice that He stopped with the words "to proclaim the acceptable year of the Lord." He did not continue to the expression, "and the day of vengeance of our God." Why? Because His First Advent ushered in the acceptable year of the Lord. His Second Advent will begin "the day of vengeance of our God."

We have a similar illustration of the two advents in Psalm 34:15-16:

15 The eyes of the Lord are on the righteous, and His ears are open to their cry. 16 The face of the Lord is against those who do evil, to cut off the remembrance of them from the earth.

When Peter quotes these verses in 1 Peter 3:12 he stops short of the words "to cut off the remembrance of them from the earth." All the rest of the quotation applies to the age in which we are now living, but this final expression looks forward to the Second Advent of Christ.

The prophet Micah foretold that Bethlehem would be the birthplace of the Messiah (Mic. 5:2):

"But you, Bethlehem Ephrathah, though you are little among the thousands of Judah, yet out of you shall come forth to Me the One to be Ruler in Israel, whose goings forth are from of old, from everlasting."

But then Micah quickly skipped over to Christ's Second Coming, when He will be great unto the ends of the earth (Mic. 5:4):

And He shall stand and feed His flock in the strength of the Lord, in the majesty of the name of the Lord His God; and they shall abide, for now He shall be great to the ends of the earth.

In Zechariah 9:9 we have an obvious prediction of Christ's triumphal entry into Jerusalem:

Rejoice greatly, O daughter of Zion! shout, O daughter of Jerusalem! Behold, Your King is coming to you; He is just and having salvation, lowly and riding on a donkey, a colt, the foal of a donkey.

But the next verse carries us forward to the Second Coming, when Christ will reign from sea to sea:

I will cut off the chariot from Ephraim and the horse from Jerusalem; the battle bow shall be cut off. He shall speak peace to the nations; His dominion shall be "from sea to sea, and from the River to the ends of the earth."

We find the two comings merged in the New Testament as well as in the Old. Take Luke 1:31-33, for example:

31 And behold, you will conceive in your womb and bring forth a Son, and shall call His name Jesus. 32 He will be great, and will be called the Son of the Highest; and the Lord God will give Him the throne of His father David. 33 And He will reign over the house of Jacob forever, and of His kingdom there will be no end.

The first verse was obviously fulfilled when Jesus was born (see Mt. 1:25). But verses 32 and 33 pass over this present Church Age to the time when Christ will return to sit on David's throne and to rule over the earth.

There is a veiled reference to the two advents in Luke 20:18:

Whoever falls on that stone will be broken; but on whomever it falls, it will grind him to powder.

In the first part of the verse, the stone (Christ) is on the earth. During His Incarnation men fell on Him and were broken. In the second half of the verse, the stone is coming down from above. When Christ comes back He will scatter the disobedient like dust.

A final and more obvious instance of the combination of the two comings is found in Hebrews 9:26, 28:

He then would have had to suffer often since the foundation of the world; but now, once at the end of the ages, He has appeared to put away sin by the sacrifice of Himself.

So Christ was offered once to bear the sins of many. To those who eagerly wait for Him He will appear a second time, apart from sin, for salvation.

He appeared once to put away sin by the sacrifice of Himself; that was His First Advent. He will appear a second time apart from sin for salvation; that is when He comes again.

20
Phases of Christ's Return

In the previous chapter we saw that it is necessary to differentiate between the first and second advents of Christ. The first belongs to history; it took place almost 2,000 years ago. The second belongs to prophecy; it is still future.

But it's also necessary to realize that the Second Coming of Christ is not a single event. Rather, it stretches over a period of time and has four stages or phases. So in this chapter we want to distinguish these phases.

In the original language of the New Testament a common word for "coming" means "a presence" or "a coming alongside" (*parousia*). It denotes an arrival and a subsequent presence. It was commonly used in connection with the arrival of the emperor and the visit that followed.

Even in the English language the word coming is used in this way. For instance, Christ's *coming* to Galilee brought healing to multitudes. Here we do not mean simply the day He arrived in Galilee, but the whole period of time He spent in that area.

So when we think of Christ's Second Coming we should think of a period of time rather than an isolated event. This period of time has four stages, as follows:

1. A beginning
2. A course
3. A manifestation
4. A climax

1. The Beginning of Christ's Coming

The beginning of Christ's Coming is called the *Rapture*, that is, the Coming of Christ for His saints. *Rapture* is from the Latin verb meaning "to snatch up," which is used in 1 Thessalonians 4:17 in the Latin Vulgate. He will come in the air, the dead in Christ will be raised, living believers will be changed, and all will go to the Father's house. This could take place at any moment, and will take place in a moment of time.

22 For as in Adam all die, even so in Christ all shall be made alive. 23 But each one in his own order: Christ the firstfruits, afterward those who are Christ's at His coming (1 Cor. 15:22-23).

13 But I do not want you to be ignorant, brethren, concerning those who have fallen asleep, lest you sorrow as others who have no hope. 14 For if we believe that Jesus died and rose again, even so God will bring with Him those who sleep in Jesus. 15 For this we say to you by the word of the Lord, that we who are alive and remain until the coming of the Lord will by no means precede those who are asleep. 16 For the Lord Himself will descend from heaven with a shout, with the voice of an archangel, and with the trumpet of God. And the dead in Christ will rise first. 17 Then we who are alive and remain shall be caught up together with them in the clouds to meet the Lord in the air. And thus we shall always be with the Lord. 18 Therefore comfort one another with these words (1 Thess. 4:13-18).

Now, brethren, concerning the coming of our Lord Jesus Christ and our gathering together to Him, we ask you... (2 Thess. 2:1).

7 Therefore be patient, brethren, until the coming of the Lord. See how the farmer waits for the precious fruit of the earth, waiting patiently for it until it receives the early and latter rain. 8 You also be patient. Establish your hearts, for the coming of the Lord is at hand (Jas. 5:7-8).

And now, little children, abide in Him, that when He appears, we may have confidence and not be ashamed before Him at His coming (1 Jn. 2:28).

Other passages which refer to the Rapture are John 14:1-4; 1 Corinthians 15:51-54; Philippians 3:20-21; 1 Thessalonians 1:10; Hebrews 9:28; 1 John 3:2; Revelation 22:7, 20.

2. The Course of Christ's Coming

The second stage, the *course* of Christ's coming, includes the Judgment Seat of Christ, when rewards will be given to believers for faithful service.

For what is our hope, or joy, or crown of rejoicing? Is it not even you in the presence of our Lord Jesus Christ at His coming? (1 Thess. 2:19).

Now may the God of peace Himself sanctify you completely; and may your whole spirit, soul, and body be preserved blameless at the coming of our Lord Jesus Christ (1 Thess. 5:23).

See also Romans 14:10-12; 1 Corinthians 3:11-15; 2 Corinthians 5:10; 2 Timothy 4:7-8.

Another event which might be included in the *course* of Christ's Coming is the Marriage Supper of the Lamb. From its location in the Book of Revelation we deduce it will take place prior to Christ's glorious reign. We include it here even though the word "coming" is not used in connection with it.

> 6 *And I heard, as it were, the voice of a great multitude, and as the sound of many waters and as the sound of mighty thunderings, saying, "Alleluia! For the Lord God Omnipotent reigns! 7 Let us be glad and rejoice and give Him glory, for the marriage of the Lamb has come, and His wife has made herself ready." 8 And to her it was granted to be arrayed in fine linen, clean and bright, for the fine linen is the righteous acts of the saints. 9 Then he said to me, "Write: 'Blessed are those who are called to the marriage supper of the Lamb!'" And he said to me, "These are the true sayings of God"* (Rev. 19:6-9).

While these events are taking place in heaven, the earth will be experiencing a time of tribulation. This will be a period of approximately seven years during which God will pour out judgments of ever-increasing intensity on the earth (Dan. 9:27; Mt. 24:4-28; Rev. 6–19). The last half of the period is known as the Great Tribulation; it will witness distress and disasters of unprecedented severity (Mt. 24:15-31).

3. The Manifestation of Christ's Coming

The third phase is the *manifestation* of Christ's coming, that is, His return to earth in power and great glory to reign as King of kings and Lord of lords. The Rapture will not be seen by the world; it will take place in a split second. But every eye will see Christ when He comes to reign. Therefore it is called the *manifestation* of His coming.

> *Now as He sat on the Mount of Olives, the disciples came to Him privately, saying, "Tell us, when will these things be? And what will be the sign of Your coming, and of the end of*

the age?" (Mt. 24:3).

For as the lightning comes from the east and flashes to the west, so also will the coming of the Son of Man be (Mt. 24:27).

But as the days of Noah were, so also will the coming of the Son of Man be (Mt. 24:37).

And [they] did not know until the flood came and took them all away, so also will the coming of the Son of Man be (Mt. 24:39).

So that He may establish your hearts blameless in holiness before our God and Father at the coming of our Lord Jesus Christ with all His saints (1 Thess. 3:13).

And then the lawless one will be revealed, whom the Lord will consume with the breath of His mouth and destroy with the brightness of His coming (2 Thess. 2:8).

For we did not follow cunningly devised fables when we made known to you the power and coming of our Lord Jesus Christ, but were eyewitnesses of His majesty (2 Pet. 1:16). (Here the apostle Peter is writing about the manifestation of Christ's coming as it was pre-pictured on the Mount of Transfiguration.)

Other references to this third stage of Christ's coming are Zechariah 14:4; Malachi 4:1-3; Acts 1:11; 2 Thessalonians 1:7-9; Jude 14; Revelation 1:7; 19:11-16.

Christ's coming *as the Son of Man* always refers to this third phase.

4. The Climax of Christ's Coming

The final stage is the *climax* of Christ's coming, the destruction of the heavens and earth by fire. It follows the thousand-year reign of Christ on earth. It is referred to in 2 Peter 3:4, 7-13:

And saying, "Where is the promise of His coming? For since the fathers fell asleep, all things continue as they were from the beginning of creation."

7 But the heavens and the earth which are now preserved by the same word, are reserved for fire until the day of judgment and perdition of ungodly men. 8 But, beloved, do not forget this one thing, that with the Lord one day is as a thousand years, and a thousand years as one day. 9 The Lord is not slack concerning His promise, as some count slackness, but is longsuffering toward us, not willing that any should perish but that all should come to repentance. 10 But the day of the Lord will come as a thief in the night, in which the heavens will pass away with a great noise, and the elements will melt with fervent heat; both the earth and the works that are in it will be burned up. 11 Therefore, since all these things will be dissolved, what manner of persons ought you to be in holy conduct and godliness, 12 looking for and hastening the coming of the day of God, because of which the heavens will be dissolved, being on fire, and the elements will melt with fervent heat? 13 Nevertheless we, according to His promise, look for new heavens and a new earth in which righteousness dwells.

In this chapter we read of scoffers who will arise in the last days, denying the probability of Christ's return. What aspect of His coming do they mean?

Are they referring to the Rapture? No. They probably know nothing about the Rapture. Are they referring to Christ's Coming to reign? No. It is apparent that they are not. The entire context indicates that what they are ridiculing is the final punishment of all evil doers by the Lord. They mean a last climactic judgment of God on the earth, or what they call "the end of the world." Their argument is that they have nothing to worry about. God hasn't intervened in history and He won't intervene in the future. So they feel free to continue in their evil words and deeds.

The apostle Peter answers their scoffing by pointing forward to the time, *after the thousand-year reign of Christ*, when the heavens and the earth as we now know them will be utterly destroyed. This climax of Christ's coming will occur *after* the Millennium and at the inauguration of the Eternal State.

"But," someone may ask, "how do you know that the first and third stages, the Rapture and Revelation, are separate events?" The answer is that they are differentiated in the

The Rapture	The Revelation
1. Christ comes to the air (1 Thess. 4:16-17).	1. He comes to the earth (Zech. 14:4).
2. He comes for His saints (1 Thess. 4:16-17).	2. He comes with His saints (1 Thess. 3:13; Jude 14).
3. The Rapture is a mystery, *i.e.*, a truth unknown in Old Testament times (1 Cor. 15:51).	3. The Revelation is not a mystery; it is the subject of many Old Testament prophecies (Ps. 72; Isa. 11; Zech. 14).
4. Christ's Coming *for* His saints is never said to be preceded by signs in the heavens.	4. Christ's Coming *with* His saints will be heralded by signs in the heavens (Mt. 24:29-30).

The Rapture	The Revelation
5. The Rapture is identified with the Day of Christ (1 Cor. 1:8; 2 Cor. 1:14; Phil. 1:6, 10).	5. The Revelation is identified with the Day of the Lord (2 Thess. 2:2 NASB).
6. The Rapture is presented as a time of blessing (1 Thess. 4:18).	6. The main emphasis of the Revelation is on judgment (2 Thess. 2:8-12).
7. The Rapture takes place in a moment, in the twinkling of an eye (1 Cor. 15:52). This strongly implies that it will not be witnessed by the world.	7. The Revelation will be visible worldwide, possibly through satellite television (Mt. 24:27; Rev. 1:7).
8. The Rapture seems to involve the Church primarily (Jn. 14:1-4; 1 Cor. 15:51-58; 1 Thess. 4:13-18).	8. The Revelation primarily involves Israel, then also the Gentile nations (Mt. 24–25).
9. Christ comes as the Bright and Morning Star (Rev. 22:16).	9. Christ comes as the Sun of Righteousness with healing in His wings (Mal. 4:2).

21

The Day of the Lord,
the Day of Christ, the Day of God

By now we should have developed some appreciation of the importance of making proper distinctions as we study the sacred Scriptures. When we come to the study of future events, we will have a headstart in understanding them if we're able to distinguish the Day of *the Lord*, the Day of *Christ*, and the Day of *God*.

The Day of the Lord

This day is certainly not a day of 24 hours, but a period of time with certain characteristics.

In the Old Testament "the Day of the Lord" was used to describe any time of judgment, desolation, and darkness (Isa. 2:12; Joel 2:1-2). It was a time when God marched forth against Israel's enemies and punished them decisively (Zeph. 3:8-12; Joel 3:14-16; Obad. 15-16; Zech. 12:8-9). It was also any occasion on which God punished His own people for their idolatry and backsliding (Joel 1:15-20; Amos 5:18; Zeph. 1:7-18). The Day of the Lord spoke basically of judgment on sin and of victory for the cause of the Lord (Joel 2:31-32).

In the New Testament, the Day of the Lord covers approximately the same period as "the times and the seasons" (Acts

141

1:7; 1 Thess. 5:1). It begins after the Rapture and includes:

1. *The Tribulation* or as it is also called, *The Time of Jacob's Trouble* (Dan. 9:27; Mt. 24:4-28; 1 Thess. 5:1-11; 2 Thess. 2:2, NASB; Rev. 6:1–19:16). This is the first phase of the Day of the Lord. It will come unexpectedly, like a thief in the night. It will also come deceptively, suddenly, destructively, inevitably, and inescapably. It is a period of approximately seven years during which God will pour out His judgments on apostate Judaism, apostate Christendom, and the Gentile nations. These judgments of ever-increasing intensity are pictured in Revelation under the symbols of seven seals, seven trumpets, and seven bowls. The last half of the Tribulation is known as the Great Tribulation. It will be the worst time of trouble that the world has ever experienced or ever will experience.

2. *The Coming of Christ with His saints* (Mal. 4:1-3; 2 Thess. 1:7-9). At the end of the Tribulation Period the Lord Jesus will return to earth with His mighty angels, "in flaming fire taking vengeance on those who do not know God, and on those who do not obey the gospel of our Lord Jesus Christ" (2 Thess. 1:8). He will destroy all His enemies before He sets up His kingdom on earth.

3. *The thousand-year reign of Christ*. This is included in the day of the Lord (Joel 3:18, cp. v. 14; Zech. 14:8-9, *cp.* v. 1). It will be a time of judgment on anyone who rebels against the Lord (Isa. 65:17-25). The King will rule with an iron rod (Rev. 19:15).

4. *The final destruction of the heavens and earth by fire* (2 Pet. 3:7, 10). At the conclusion of Christ's millennial

reign, the heavens and the earth will pass away with a great noise and the elements will melt with fervent heat. This is the final phase of the Day of the Lord.

The Day of Christ

Whereas the Day of the Lord is a time of judgment on a world that has rejected God's Son, the Day of *Christ* is a time of blessing for those who have trusted Him and who are thus members of His Church. It is the same as the Day of the Lord Jesus, the Day of Jesus Christ, and the Day of our Lord Jesus Christ. There are two main features of this Day:

1. *The Rapture of the saints* (1 Cor. 5:5; Phil. 1:6, 10). The dead in Christ will be raised. Living believers will be changed. Together they will be caught up to meet the Lord in the air and to return with Him to the Father's house in heaven.

2. *The Judgment Seat of Christ* (1 Cor. 1:8; 2 Cor. 1:14; Phil. 2:16). Believers will appear before "the Bema"—the judgment seat—for review and reward. It will not be a question of their salvation but of their service. Rewards will be given for all that meets Christ's approval. Those who have wasted their lives will suffer loss, but they themselves will be saved, though "as through fire" (1 Cor. 3:15).

Through an unfortunate textual choice in the King James tradition, "the day of *Christ*" appears in 2 Thessalonians 2:2, whereas most Bible scholars believe it should read "the Day of the *Lord*." Because of the intense trial which they were experiencing, the Thessalonian believers thought the judgments of the Day of the Lord had already begun. Paul assures them that

143

two events will precede the inauguration of the Day of the Lord—a worldwide falling away (apostasy) from the faith, and the revelation of the Man of Sin—the Antichrist.

The Thessalonians would have had no reason to fear the coming of *the Day of Christ*. For them that would have meant being rescued from trials forever.

The Day of God

The Day of God is not to be confused with the Day of the Lord or the Day of Christ. It is the day of God's final triumph. It will take place after all evil has been forever put down, and after the heavens and the earth have been destroyed by fire (2 Pet. 3:12). For all practical purposes, the Day of God is the same as the eternal state.

22
Double Fulfillments

When we come to the study of the prophetic Scriptures, one of the most helpful keys is to realize that some prophecies have more than one fulfillment. It's not unusual to find a prediction that has a preliminary, partial fulfillment and then later a full, final accomplishment. This is known as the "law of double reference."

Outpouring of the Spirit

The classic example is Joel's prophecy concerning the pouring out of the Spirit of God:

> 28 *And it shall come to pass afterward that I will pour out My Spirit on all flesh; Your sons and your daughters shall prophesy, your old men shall dream dreams, your young men shall see visions. 29 And also on My menservants and on My maidservants I will pour out My Spirit in those days. 30 And I will show wonders in the heavens and in the earth, blood and fire and pillars of smoke. 31 The sun shall be turned into darkness, and the moon into blood, before the coming of the great and awesome day of the Lord. 32 And it shall come to pass that whoever calls on the name of the Lord shall be saved...* (Joel 2:28-32a).

When the apostle Peter quoted this passage on the day of

Pentecost (Acts 2:14-21), he said, "...this is what was spoken by the prophet Joel." But he could not have meant that it was a *complete* fulfillment, since some of the things that Joel mentioned didn't occur at Pentecost.

The Spirit was not poured out on *all flesh*, but only on *three thousand Jews*. There were no wonders in the heavens—the sun was not turned to darkness, nor the moon to blood. Not all the signs on earth occurred, either—such as blood and fire and vapor of smoke.

This means that Pentecost was an early and incomplete fulfillment of Joel's prophecy. Its total realization will take place at the Second Advent of Christ. His coming will be preceded by the predicted signs and followed by the pouring out of His Spirit on all humanity in the millennial earth.

Remarkable Births

We have another illustration of the "law of double reference" in the famous "virgin" passage of Isaiah 7:14:

Therefore the Lord himself will give you a sign. Behold, a young woman [Hebrew *almah*] *shall conceive and bear a son, and shall call his name Immanuel* (RSV).

The prophecy obviously had an immediate meaning for King Ahaz, namely, that a child would be born and named "God with us," implying that victory was near. Before the child would be old enough to discern good and evil, the Syria-Israel alliance would be crushed, and within a few more years the child would be living on the fat of the land (v. 15).

But the *complete* unfolding of the verse came with the birth of Christ.

22 *Now all this was done that it might be fulfilled which was*

spoken by the Lord through the prophet, saying:
23 *"Behold, the virgin shall be with child, and bear a Son, and they shall call His name Immanuel," which is translated, "God with us" (Mt. 1:22-23).*

The Hebrew word *almah* used by Isaiah allows for the double fulfillment. It can mean a young woman or a virgin. But the Greek word *parthenos* used in Matthew can only mean virgin.

Triumphal Entries

A third example of dual fulfillment is found in Psalm 118:26a:

Blessed is he who comes in the name of the Lord.

On the first Palm Sunday, when Jesus rode into Jerusalem, the crowd shouted,

...Hosanna to the Son of David! "Blessed is He who comes in the name of the Lord!"... (Mt. 21:9).

But we know that this did not exhaust the prophecy, because in His later lament over Jerusalem, the Lord Jesus said,

For I say to you, you shall see Me no more again till you say, "Blessed is He who comes in the name of the Lord" (Mt. 23:39).

The final fulfillment will occur when the Savior returns to earth in power and glory to a people who will welcome Him as Messiah and King.

Destructions of Jerusalem

Still another illustration of a prophecy which has two fulfillments concerns the destruction of Jerusalem. Jesus predicted the desolation of the city in Luke 21:20-24. His words obviously came to pass in AD 70, when Titus and his Roman legions sacked the city and leveled the Temple. But Jerusalem's woes are not all past. It's clear from Revelation 11:2 that the Gentiles will, sad to say, again trample on the holy city for forty-two months during the Tribulation period.

Rebellions Against Christ

Psalm 2:1-2 is quoted in Acts 4:25-26:

25 ... 'Why did the nations rage, and the people plot vain things? 26 The kings of the earth took their stand, and the rulers were gathered together against the Lord and against His Christ.'

In Acts 4:27, the words are applied to the crucifixion of Christ:

For truly against Your holy Servant Jesus, whom You anointed, both Herod and Pontius Pilate, with the Gentiles and the people of Israel, were gathered together...

That was a preliminary and partial fulfillment of the Psalmist's words. They will have a still further fulfillment at the close of the Tribulation when world rulers will unite in a futile attempt to prevent Christ from taking the reins of universal government.

Regatherings of Israel

A final example of the law of double reference can be found in prophecies dealing with the regathering of Israel (Isa. 43:5-7; Jer. 16:14-15; Ezek. 36:8-11; 37:21). These prophecies had a very partial fulfillment when a remnant of the Jews returned from Babylonian captivity to Israel, as described in Ezra and Nehemiah. But the main event is still future. Any past regatherings have been only a trickle. During the time of Jacob's trouble, God will bring His chosen earthly people back to Israel from all over the world (Mt. 24:31; Deut. 30:3-4; Ezek. 36:24-32; 37:11-14). Then and only then will the prophecies be completely and finally fulfilled.

23
Seven Judgments

In studying the Bible, it's important to realize that there are many different judgments, and that these must be distinguished as to the people, time, and places involved, the basis of the judgment, and the results. Many people, for instance, think that the Judgment of the Nations is the same as the Judgment of the Great White Throne. Careful examination will reveal that they are very different.

Certainly the discerning student will see that there is no such thing as one "general judgment" when believers and unbelievers stand before God and hear their verdict.

Here we deal with seven of the more important judgments found in God's Word.

The Judgment of Human Sin

At Calvary, God judged sin when the Lord Jesus bore its penalty in His body on the Cross. The Savior died for the sins of the world:

> 14 *For the love of Christ compels us, because we judge thus: that **if One died for all**, then all died; 15 and **He died for all**, that those who live should live no longer for themselves, but for Him who died for them and rose again* (2 Cor 5:14-15, emphasis added).

*And He Himself is the propitiation for our sins, and not for ours only but also for **the whole world*** (1 Jn. 2:2, emphasis added).

When He died, He effectively paid the penalty of sin. His shed blood met all the claims of God's righteousness against sin. He provided a way by which God could save ungodly sinners without condoning sin or compromising His holiness. His redemptive work was of infinite power to put away sin.

However, His work at the Cross does not automatically save everyone. His substitutionary work was *sufficient* to cover the sins of all the world, but only those who repent and trust the Lord Jesus become beneficiaries of that work.

When a person does accept Christ as His Lord and Savior, he is forever free from the guilt and penalty of sin. He will never come into eternal judgment for his sins, because Jesus bore the judgment, and God will not demand payment twice. The believer receives once-for-all, judicial forgiveness through faith.

The Self-Judgment of the Believer

Once a person is saved, he is required to carry on a kind of self-judgment in his own life. This means that he must confess and forsake sin as soon as he is conscious that it has happened. This is what Paul is referring to in 1 Corinthians 11:27-32:

27 Therefore whoever eats this bread or drinks this cup of the Lord in an unworthy manner will be guilty of the body and blood of the Lord. 28 But let a man examine himself, and so let him eat of the bread and drink of the cup. 29 For he who eats and drinks in an unworthy manner eats and drinks judgment to himself, not discerning the Lord's body.

30 For this reason many are weak and sick among you, and many sleep. 31 For if we would judge ourselves, we would not be judged. 32 But when we are judged, we are chastened by the Lord, that we may not be condemned with the world.

We judge sin in our lives when we acknowledge it as being there, then confess it and put it away. This self-judgment should go on throughout our lives. Otherwise we endure the Father's chastening, as described in Hebrews 12:3-15.

The apostle Paul realized that if he did not judge sin in his life, he would be disqualified for Christian service.

But I discipline my body and bring it into subjection, lest, when I have preached to others, I myself should become disqualified (1 Cor. 9:27).

The Judgment Seat of Christ

In considering the Judgment Seat of Christ, we should not think of a criminal trial but rather of a flower show or an athletic event. The Lord is not there to convict and condemn the guilty. He is there to award *prizes*! It's not a court scene but a time of review and reward.

All believers will appear at this Judgment Seat, also called the *Bema* (the Greek word).

...For we shall all stand before the judgment seat of Christ (Rom. 14:10c).

It is clear that this great event takes place in eternity, after the resurrection of the saints. Believers will then be in their glorified bodies.

The service of God's people will be evaluated:

For we must all appear before the judgment seat of Christ,

153

that each one may receive the things done in the body, according to what he has done, whether good or bad (2 Cor. 5:10).

Some will be rewarded, and some will suffer loss:

13 *Each one's work will become clear; for the Day will declare it, because it will be revealed by fire; and the fire will test each one's work, of what sort it is.* 14 *If anyone's work which he has built on it endures, he will receive a reward.* 15 *If anyone's work is burned, he will suffer loss...* (1 Cor. 3:13-15a).

Yet the last part of v. 15 makes it clear that the person's salvation is never at risk in this judgment:

...but he himself will be saved, yet so as through fire.

The Judgment of Israel

No nation has ever endured the hatred, the mistreatment, the persecution, and the pogroms that the Jewish people have. The Holocaust is only one chapter in a heart-rending record of sorrow, suffering, and death.

Yet, sad to say, the end is not yet. After the Rapture of the Church, Israel and the nations will go through a seven-year period of tribulation, the last half of which is a time of unprecedented trouble. Jeremiah calls it "the time of Jacob's trouble" (Jer. 30:7) and the Lord actually uses the words "great tribulation":

For then there will be great tribulation, such as has not been since the beginning of the world until this time, no, nor ever shall be (Mt. 24:21).

At the end of this time, the Messiah will appear. The nation will be regathered and the Lord will plead His case with the people face to face in a place He calls "the wilderness of the peoples" (Ezek. 20:33-44).

One of the chief crimes that will be dealt with will be the worship of the Antichrist during the Tribulation. The Lord Jesus predicted that much of the nation would fall into this worst form of idolatry:

I have come in My Father's name, and you do not receive Me; if another comes in his own name, him you will receive (Jn. 5:43).

Malachi gives an enlarged list of sins that will be dealt with by the King (Mal. 2:1–3:5).

It is clear that all who rebel against the Messiah-King will be destroyed before the Kingdom is inaugurated, while all who submit to His rule will enter His glorious kingdom and enjoy His reign of peace and prosperity for 1,000 years:

26 *And so all* [believing] *Israel will be saved, as it is written, "The Deliverer will come out of Zion, and He will turn away ungodliness from Jacob; 27 For this is My covenant with them, when I take away their sins"* (Rom. 11:26-27).

The Judgment of the Nations

The principal passage dealing with the judgment of the Gentile nations is Matthew 25:31-46. This court is convened at the Second Coming of the Lord. The Judge is the Son of Man, that is, Jesus Himself.

When the Son of Man comes in His glory, and all the holy angels with Him, then He will sit on the throne of His glory (v. 31).

The prophet Joel makes it clear that Israel's treatment by the Gentiles is a prominent feature of this judgment (Joel 3:2). Those nations which protect and befriend Christ's Jewish brethren during the Tribulation are called sheep in Matthew 25. Those which withhold food, drink, clothing, hospitality, and which refuse even social contact with the ill and the imprisoned are the goat nations.

The sheep nations will "inherit the kingdom prepared... from the foundation of the world" (v. 34). The goat nations will hear their sentence, "Depart from Me, you cursed, into the everlasting fire prepared for the devil and his angels" (v. 41).

And these will go away into everlasting punishment, but the righteous into eternal life (v. 46).

Some people have trouble with the idea of *nations*[1] being saved or lost. They think of salvation as being exclusively an individual matter. This should not be a problem. All down through history, God has dealt with nations as well as with individuals. If the majority of people in a country or district are rebels against God, He characteristically first delivers His own people, then pours out His wrath on the mass of the population. Sodom is an example of this. And so is the flood, but on a grander scale.

The Judgment of Angels

Without fully satisfying our curiosity, the Bible tells us that some fallen angels have been incarcerated, awaiting their final judgment:

For if God did not spare the angels who sinned, but cast them down to hell and delivered them into chains of darkness, to be reserved for judgment... (2 Pet. 2:4).

And the angels who did not keep their proper domain, but left their own abode, He has reserved in everlasting chains under darkness for the judgment of the great day (Jude 6).

We know only too well that there are other evil angels (generally equated with demons) that are still at large. When will the judgment of all fallen angels take place?

During His reign on earth, the Messiah-King will put "an end to all rule and all authority and power," and "put all enemies under His feet" (1 Cor. 15:24-25). This doubtless includes the subjugation of principalities, powers, and spiritual wickedness in heavenly places.

Since believers will be reigning with Him, they will share in the judging of angels. Perhaps this explains Paul's enigmatic question in 1 Corinthians 6:3: "Do you not know that we shall judge angels?"

Satan's final judgment takes place at the end of the Millennium and before the Judgment of the Great White Throne:

The devil, who deceived them, was cast into the lake of fire and brimstone where the beast and the false prophet are. And they will be tormented day and night forever and ever (Rev. 20:10).

Since fallen angels acknowledge Satan as their leader, it is reasonable to believe that they will be condemned for sharing in his rebellion against God (Isa. 14:12-17; Ezek. 28:12-19) and will share in his doom in the lake of fire.

The Judgment of the Great White Throne

John "saw a great white throne and Him who sat on it, from whose face the earth and the heaven fled away" (Rev. 20:11).

The throne is great because of the One who sits on it and because of the tremendous issues at stake. Its whiteness speaks of the purity of its judgment. This judgment takes place in eternity, after the world as we know it has been dissolved by fervent heat (2 Pet. 3:10).

"And I saw the dead, small and great, standing before God" (Rev. 20:12a). These are the wicked dead of all the ages. The reason they are standing here is because they did not put their faith in the Lord. Unbelief is the great, damning sin.

...he who does not believe is condemned already, because he has not believed in the name of the only begotten Son of God (Jn. 3:18b).

...he who does not believe the Son shall not see life, but the wrath of God abides on him (Jn. 3:36b).

Now two books are opened to determine the degree of their punishment:

...and books were opened. And another book was opened, which is the Book of Life. And the dead were judged according to their works, by the things which were written in the books (Rev. 20:12b).

Their doom is sealed by the fact that their names are not written in the Book of Life, which means that they never repented and believed in Christ as their Savior. But there will be degrees of punishment in hell just as there will be degrees of reward in heaven. Their works determine the measure of their guilt. A serial rapist, for instance, will suffer more than a refined neighbor who lived a fairly decent life (but who, sadly, was never converted).

The body, here represented as Death, and the spirit and soul, symbolized by Hades—in other words, the complete person, is cast into the lake of fire:

Then Death and Hades were cast into the lake of fire. This is the second death (Rev. 20:14).

No believer will appear at the Judgment of the Great White Throne. It is only for those who spurned God's offer of mercy and hence did not have their names inscribed in the Lamb's Book of Life.

Endnote

1 In addition, it should be noted that the word translated "nations" (*ethne*) can equally well be translated "Gentiles," and often is so rendered.

24
Hades & Hell

There is a difference between Hades and hell. The words in the original language of the New Testament are different and have different meanings. They cannot be used interchangeably.[1] Hades is temporary whereas hell is eternal. Hades is the same as *Sheol* in the Old Testament, whereas hell is the same as Gehenna and the lake of fire. Hades has been likened to a city jail where prisoners are held for trial. It is a holding tank. Hell is the federal penitentiary where the sentence is carried out.

Hades

First, let's consider Hades. Sometimes it seems to refer to a place of suffering, sometimes to the grave, and at other times to the disembodied state. If it is a place, there is no indication as to its location. The fullest treatment of Hades is in Luke 16:19-31 where we read that an unbelieving rich man lifted up his eyes in Hades. This man's body was obviously in the grave and his soul was in Hades. Yet in that conscious condition, he had intelligence, memory, and the power to look across a yawning chasm and see heaven, or paradise. He was suffering torment from the heat and from thirst. He had evangelistic zeal because he wanted someone to testify to his five brothers so that they would not end up in this place of torment. Here

161

Hades is specifically said to be a *place* of torment. There is no escape from it.

But in Acts 2:27, it is not so much a place as a state or condition. Peter quotes Psalm 16:10 and refers it to the resurrection of Christ:

Because You will not leave my soul in Hades, nor will You allow Your Holy One to see corruption.

Hades here could not be a place because when the Lord Jesus died, His spirit and soul went to paradise,[2] which is the same as the third heaven,[3] the dwelling place of God. But it could refer to the disembodied state. God did not allow His soul to remain in that condition, neither did He allow His Holy One, that is, the body of the Savior, to see corruption. The expression "His Holy One" must refer to the body because that is the only part of man that corrupts at the time of death. Peter boldly announced that the Lord's soul was not left in Hades (Acts 2:31). On the third day His spirit and soul were reunited with His glorified body.

Another passage that pictures Hades as the disembodied state is Revelation 20:13-14:

13 The sea gave up the dead who were in it, and Death and Hades delivered up the dead who were in them. And they were judged, each one according to his works. 14 Then Death and Hell were cast into the lake of fire. This is the second death.

The scene is the final judgment of the wicked. The Lord Jesus Christ is the Judge, the One who has the keys of Death and Hades (Rev. 1:18). Death here refers to their bodies, and Hades refers to their spirits and souls. The spirits and souls of all unbelievers are reunited with their bodies at the Judgment

162

of the Great White Throne, and the complete persons are cast into the lake of fire.

Another passage in which Hades seems to refer to the disembodied state is 1 Corinthians 15:55:

O Death, where is your sting? O Hades, where is your victory?

This is a taunt song that will be sung by believers at the coming of Christ. As their bodies rise from the grave, they will remind Death that, yes, it held them for a while, but it could not keep them! And although Hades succeeded in holding their spirits and souls separate from the bodies, its victory was short lived.

In Revelation 6:8, we are introduced to a rider on a pale horse named Death, with Hades following with him. The rest of the verse explains that Death and Hades were given power to kill a fourth of earth's population. Here again, Death and Hades figuratively depict the separation of the soul and the spirit from the body, which is what death is.

Sometimes the word *Hades* is used as a metaphor to picture the depth of humiliation. For example, the city of Capernaum was lifted up to heaven in privilege. But it didn't appreciate the presence of the Son of God, and so it would be brought down to Hades in shame and destruction (Mt. 11:23; Lk. 10:15).

The only other reference to Hades is in Matthew 16:18 where Jesus guaranteed that the gates of Hades would not prevail against the Church which He would establish. No attack on the Church would ultimately succeed, whereas the Church's victory against Hades is assured.

Hell

Of the twelve occurrences of the word *hell* in the New

163

Testament, eleven of them came from the lips of the Lord Jesus, who is the most compassionate of all people. The twelfth occurrence is by our Lord's half-brother, James.

What may we know about this terrible place? It was not prepared for man but for the devil and his angels (Mt. 25:41). God does not elect anyone to this judgment; by refusing God's grace, people choose hell for themselves. It's a place where there is weeping, wailing, and gnashing of teeth (Mt. 8:12; 22:13; 24:51; 25:30; Lk. 13:28). It is said of the occupants of hell that their worm (torment) does not die (cease) and the fire is not quenched (Mk. 9:46). The smoke of their torment ascends forever and ever (Rev. 14:11).

Jesus repeatedly emphasized that it is better to enter into life with parts of the body missing than to be cast into hell with the body intact (Mt. 5:29-30; 18:9; Mk. 9:43, 45, 47). Of course, this does not mean that there will be amputees in heaven. Rather it says that it is better to exercise rigid discipline over the appetites of the body in this life than to cater to its lusts and be doomed eternally.

Believers should not fear those who can destroy[4] the body, but rather fear Him who is able to destroy both soul and body in hell (Mt. 10:28; Lk. 12:5).

Anyone who manifests a settled hatred of his brother by calling him a fool is in danger of hell fire (Mt. 5:22). Evil speech is hellish in its character (Jas. 3:6). The sins of the Pharisees made them fit subjects for hell (Mt. 23:15, 33).

Tartaros

The Greek word *tartaros*,[5] translated *hell* in 2 Peter 2:4, seems to have a specialized meaning for fallen angels who sinned. In *tartaros* they are delivered into chains of darkness to be reserved for judgment.

Purgatory

According to the Roman Catholic Church, "purgatory" is a state or place of punishment after death where a person who dies in God's grace may make atonement for the "temporal punishment" due to sin and thus gain entrance into heaven. The fires of purgatory are supposed to have a purifying effect on the soul. It is also alleged that the time in purgatory may be shortened by the prayers of the living and by masses that are offered in their behalf. The Bible knows nothing of such a state or place as purgatory. The word is never mentioned and the teaching is completely contrary to the truth of full salvation by grace through faith in our Lord Jesus Christ.

Endnotes

1 Some translations of the Bible fail to differentiate between hell and Hades. In the King James Version, for example, the word for Hades was uniformly translated *hell* except in 1 Corinthians 15:55, where it was translated grave. *Hades* is from the Greek word for "unseen" [world]. *Hell* is an Anglo-Saxon word that translates the Hebrew name *Gehenna*. To make the horrors of eternal punishment vivid to His hearers our Lord used a term for a place of continual burning of refuse.

2 Luke 23:43

3 2 Cor. 12:2, compare v. 4.

4 The word *destroy* does not mean annihilation or the loss of being, but rather the loss of well-being, the nonfulfillment of the purpose for which a person or thing was created. For example, the wineskins that burst in Matthew 9:1 were not annihilated, but *ruined* as to their reason for being made.

5 Also spelled in the Latin manner, *Tartarus*.

25
Mysteries of Scripture

The New Testament presents us with a series of mysteries. The danger is not so much to confuse them as to fail to understand them. We will therefore devote this lesson to a short summary of the meanings of the various mysteries.

Definition

A *mystery* is a truth which has never before been revealed, which man could not arrive at by his own intellect, and which has now been revealed by God to men. The word is just the anglicized form of the Greek word *mysterion* used in the original.

The Mysteries of the Kingdom of Heaven
Matthew 13:3-50

In Matthew 13:11 we read of "the mysteries of the kingdom of heaven." They are presented in that chapter in the form of seven parables.

In the early chapters of Matthew we find the Lord Jesus presenting Himself to Israel as Messiah-King. But in chapter 12 the religious leaders rejected Him by accusing Him of performing miracles in the power of Beelzebub (the Devil). So now that the King has been rejected, the kingdom will take a different form. That is what is found in Matthew 13. These seven parables give a description of the kingdom in its *interim* form—during the time between the rejection of the King and His return to reign over the earth. The King is absent, but His kingdom is found wherever people profess to be His subjects. There is both profession and reality. This, of course, is the period of time in which we all live.

At the close of this interim period the wheat will be separated from the tares, the true from the false. The King's true subjects will enjoy the blessings of His millennial reign; the false will be destroyed.

The Mystery of Israel's Blindness
Romans 11:25

Because of Israel's rejection of the King, God has caused a judicial blindness to come upon the Jewish nation. This partly explains the great difficulty which Jewish people have in accepting Jesus as their Messiah, and the relatively small number who are saved. But this blindness is neither total nor final. More and more Jewish people (especially in those countries where they have generally been well treated) are coming to see that Jesus is the One of whom the prophets spoke. And the blindness will continue only until the "fullness of the Gentiles" has come, that is, until the Lord takes His largely Gentile bride home to be with Himself. Then a believing remnant out of Israel will turn to Christ.

The Mystery of the Rapture
1 Corinthians 15:51-52

Up to this time in human history it was always believed that everyone would die sooner or later. But now the apostle Paul makes the startling announcement that not all believers will die. Those who are living at the time of the Rapture will go to heaven without dying. They will be changed—that is, they will receive glorified bodies—and they will never experience death. Those who have died in Christ will be raised and taken to heaven with the living saints. Further details are found in 1 Thessalonians 4:13-18.

The Mystery of the Church
Romans 16:25; Ephesians 3:4-5

The Church was a truth kept secret since the world began (Rom. 16:25) but revealed to the apostles and prophets of the New Testament period (Eph. 3:5). This mystery embraces such important features as:

1. The headship of Christ (Col. 1:18).
2. The membership of all believers (1 Cor. 12:13).
3. The fact that believing Gentiles share equally with believing Jews, that Christ is their hope of glory too, and that the ancient enmity between Jew and Gentile has been abolished in Christ (Eph. 3:6; Col. 1:26-27; Eph. 2:14-15).
4. The Church as the body of Christ (1 Cor. 12:12-13).
5. The Church as the bride of Christ (Eph. 5:25-27; 31-32).
6. The Church as a display of the manifold wisdom of God to principalities and powers in heavenly places (Eph. 3:10).
7. God's purpose to make Christ the Head of a redeemed universe (Eph. 1:9-10), with the Church reigning as His bride and sharing His glory forever.

"This mystery among the Gentiles" in Colossians 1:27 is defined as "Christ in you, the hope of glory." This is the same mystery as the Church; it emphasizes that Christ is the hope of glory for believing Gentiles as well as believing Jews—all now have the same standing before God in Christ.

In Colossians 2:2 (NASB) the mystery of God is identified as Christ. We understand this to refer to the mystical body of Christ, with Christ Himself as the Head and all believers comprising the body.

Other passages that refer to the mystery of the Church are Ephesians 6:19 and Colossians 4:3. There is a sense in which this mystery of the Church is the capstone of scriptural revelation. The apostle Paul fulfilled the Word of God when he passed on this truth (Col. 1:25). It was not chronologically the last part of the Bible to be written but, as far as the revelation of important new truth, it was the climax.

The Mystery of Lawlessness
2 Thessalonians 2:7-8

The only reference to the "mystery of lawlessness" is in 2 Thessalonians 2:7-8. There Paul says that "the mystery of lawlessness is already at work; only He who now restrains will do so until He is taken out of the way. And then the lawless one will be revealed...." Even in the early days of the Church a spirit of lawlessness was already operating. There were many antichrists. But the full development of lawlessness was restrained by an unnamed Person (whom we believe to be the Holy Spirit). When that restraining Person is removed (the Holy Spirit will be taken away as the permanent Indweller at the Rapture), then the Man of Lawlessness, the Antichrist, will stride onto the stage of history. He will be the very embodiment of sin and lawlessness. The world will never before have seen such a concentration of wickedness in any human being.

The Mystery of the Faith
1 Timothy 3:9

The "mystery of the faith" refers to the body of Christian

doctrine, or what we call the Christian faith. It is called a mystery because so many of its truths were completely unknown in Old Testament times.

The Mystery of Godliness
1 Timothy 3:16

1 Timothy 3:16 reads:

And without controversy, great is the mystery of godliness: God was manifested in the flesh, justified in the Spirit, seen by angels, preached among the Gentiles, believed on in the world, received up in glory.

The Person of the Godhead described can fit only one person—our Lord Jesus Christ. Up to the time that Christ came into the world, no one had ever seen perfect godliness in a human life. But the Lord Jesus came and gave a practical demonstration of what an absolutely godly person is like.

When Paul says that the mystery of godliness is "great" (Greek: *mega*), he doesn't mean that it's deeply mysterious, but rather that the truth of the Person of Christ is marvelous and wonderful.

The mystery of godliness stands in contrast to the mystery of lawlessness. The first presents a Man who perfectly embodies piety. The second presents the living embodiment of sin. It is the stark contrast between Christ and Antichrist.

The Mystery of the Seven Stars
Revelation 1:20

This mystery is clearly defined. The seven stars in John's vision are the angels (or messengers: the word can be translated either way) of the seven churches of Asia. The seven golden lampstands are the seven churches. In the next two chapters, the Lord addresses letters to the angels of the seven churches. These letters may be understood in three different ways.

1. They were seven literal letters written to seven literal, historic churches that existed in John's day. Nearly all accept this to be true.

2. They describe conditions which may be found in the Church worldwide at any particular time in its history. This also seems to be a clear application to most Bible students.

3. They give a chronological preview of conditions in the professing Church from the days of the apostles to the end of the Church era. Not all accept this view, but the parallels are remarkable.

The Mystery of God
Revelation 10:7

When the seventh trumpet of Revelation 10 sounds, the mystery of God will be fulfilled. The sounding of the seventh trumpet is accompanied by loud voices in heaven saying, "The kingdoms of this world have become the kingdoms of our Lord and of His Christ, and He shall reign forever and ever" (Rev. 11:15). From this we know that the seventh trumpet sounds at the close of the Great Tribulation, when Christ returns to earth to reign (Rev. 11:17). At that time the Lord's faithful Tribulation saints will be rewarded and His enemies will be destroyed (v. 18).

The mystery of God will then be fulfilled. The evil which has been so persistent and apparently triumphant will be put down. God's seeming indifference to man's wickedness and

His apparent inaction will have ended. As W. A. Criswell says, "The long delay of our Lord in taking the kingdom unto Himself and in establishing righteousness on the earth will be over." F. W. Grant put it this way: "The mystery of God is forever finished; the glory of God shines like the sun; faith is completely justified, the murmur of doubt forever silenced."

The Mystery of Babylon
Revelation 17:5-7

Babylon the Great is pictured in Revelation 17 as a harlot sitting on a beast with seven heads and ten horns. She is named "*Babylon the Great, the Mother of Harlots and of the Abominations of the earth.*" The explanation of the mystery is given in verses 8-18. The woman is a great city that reigns over the kings of the earth (v. 18). The beast is an empire that in turn existed at one time, passed out of existence, will be revived, and will be destroyed (v. 8). The seven heads are seven kings of this empire (v. 9). The ten horns are ten kings who will be federated with this empire (v. 12). The harlot rides on the back of the beast for awhile, but is then destroyed by it (v. 16). The empire itself will eventually be destroyed by the Lord (v. 14).

Our interpretation of this mystery is as follows. The woman represents a great religious and economic system which will have its headquarters in Rome; it will be a world church with vast financial resources. The beast represents the revived Roman Empire in a ten kingdom form, somewhat along the geographical lines of the European Community.

After supporting the world church for a time, the ruler of the revived Roman Empire and the ten kings who are his allies will turn against the system and destroy it. (Further details concerning Babylon and her destruction in Rev. 18.)

Conclusion

There are four other references to mysteries in the New Testament.

In 1 Corinthians 2:7, Paul says that he and the other apostles spoke "the wisdom of God in a mystery." Then he explains that he means truths which were hidden to previous generations but which have now been revealed through the Holy Spirit.

He and the other apostles were "stewards of the mysteries of God" (1 Cor. 4:1). Here again the word is used in a general sense to cover all the new truth of the Christian dispensation.

But he reminds us in 1 Corinthians 13:2 that it's not enough to know all mysteries and all knowledge. If we don't have love, we are nothing.

And finally, in 1 Corinthians 14:2, Paul explains that if someone speaks in a foreign language with no interpreter present, he benefits no one, even though he may be speaking the most profound mysteries.

26
Aspects of the Glories of Christ

When we speak of the glories of Christ, we refer to His supreme excellences, whether in His Person, His position, or His work. It may mean His moral and spiritual perfections which are seen by the eye of faith through the Word of God. Or it may mean His physical magnificence and splendor in heaven at the present time or when He returns to earth as King of kings and Lord of lords.

It's impossible to number the glories of the Lord Jesus. They exhaust human vocabulary. In this chapter we confine ourselves to seven aspects of that glory as they are found in the sacred Scriptures.

His Original, Personal Glory as God the Son

This refers to all the excellencies and perfections of Christ's deity. It's a glory that is eternal and inherent. He is no less than the brightness of God's glory (Heb. 1:3). The Lord Jesus could neither empty Himself of this glory nor lay it aside. It is an intrinsic part of His being. It includes all His marvelous attributes and virtues. In coming to earth, *He veiled this glory* in a body of flesh, but it was there all the time, and shone out at intervals, such as at His transfiguration (Mt. 17:1-8; Mk. 9:1-8; Lk. 9:28-36).

His Positional Glory in Heaven

From all eternity, the Lord Jesus occupied a position of indescribable honor and splendor. He was the daily delight of His Father and the object of angelic worship. But when the redemption of humanity was at stake, He did not feel that He must hold on to that position at all costs. Instead, *He emptied Himself* of it (Phil. 2:7a, literal translation), took the form of a servant, and came in the likeness of man. It was doubtless this positional glory that Charles Wesley was thinking about when he wrote, "Mild He lays His glory by, born that man no more may die."[1]

It is extremely important to realize that the Savior's self-emptying refers only to His *position* in heaven and not to His *Person*. A prince could leave a palace to live in a jungle, but there is no way in which he could relinquish his personhood.

In John 17:5, the Savior prayed, "And now, O Father, glorify Me together with Yourself, with the glory which I had with You before the world was." In other words, He was asking for the restoration of that positional glory which He had with the Father but laid aside by coming to earth.

The Glory of His Life on Earth as the Son of Man

As a man on earth, the Lord Jesus was glorious in the miracles He performed. Thus we read, "This beginning of signs Jesus did in Cana of Galilee, and manifested His glory" (Jn. 2:11a). He was glorious in the perfections of His character. He knew no sin, He did no sin, there was no sin in Him (2 Cor. 5:21; 1 Pet. 2:22; 1 Jn. 3:5). He was so morally perfect that He could do nothing in self-will. He could do only those things which the Father gave Him to do (Jn. 5:19),[2] and He could speak only the word which the Father gave Him to speak (Jn. 13:50; 17:8). Pilate had to admit he could find no fault in Him

(Lk. 23:14, 22; Jn. 18:38; 19:4, 6). Herod's decision was that Christ had done nothing worthy of death (Lk. 23:15). The dying thief testified that Jesus had done nothing wrong (Lk. 23:41). Even Judas confessed that he had betrayed "innocent" blood (Mt. 27:4).

The Savior was not only glorious in His sinlessness; He was glorious in His speech. The people of Nazareth marveled at the gracious words that proceeded from His mouth (Lk. 4:22). Officers who were sent to arrest Him had to confess, "No man ever spoke like this Man!" (Jn. 7:46). He was glorious in His perfect humanity. This is known as the moral glory of our Lord Jesus Christ.

His Acquired Glories

Had our Lord remained in heaven, He never could have been our Savior. But by going to the Cross and rising from the tomb, He *became perfect as Savior*. Thus we read:

For it was fitting for Him, for whom are all things and by whom are all things, in bringing many sons to glory, to make the author of their salvation perfect through suffer-ings (Heb. 2:10).

And having been perfected, He became the author of eternal salvation to all who obey Him (Heb. 5:9).

Clearly He could not be made perfect as to His *Person*. He always has been perfect in that respect. But He could and did become the perfect *Savior*.

The Lord alluded to this acquired glory when, in anticipation of Calvary, He said:

...The hour has come that the Son of Man should be glorified (Jn. 12:23b).

177

In addition to His acquired glory as the perfect Savior, the Lord Jesus gained other honors by His incarnation and sacrificial work. Apart from His incarnation, He never could have become the Messiah, because the Christ must be a descendant of David. Apart from Calvary, He never could be High Priest, Advocate, Mediator, Intercessor, Redeemer, Good Shepherd, Heir of all things, Judge, or the Head of the Church. He never could have had the Name that is above every name or be the First-begotten from the dead. Any titles that are the fruit of His incarnation, death, burial, and resurrection are *acquired* glories.

He refers to another instance of His acquired glory in John 17:10:

And all Mine are Yours, and Yours are Mine, and I am glorified in them.

That He should be glorified in His saints is something that could only happen as a result of His work at Calvary.

In 2 Thessalonians 1:10a, Paul links this in a special way with the Lord's second coming:

...When He comes, in that Day, to be glorified in His saints and to be admired among all those who believe...

The Glory of His Resurrection and Ascension

Again in John 17:1, our Lord is speaking as if Calvary had already come. He prays that the Father might glorify Him, that is, by raising Him from the dead, so that the Son, in turn, might glorify the Father.

We have a similar passage in John 13:31-32:

30 So, when he [Judas] had gone out, Jesus said, "Now the Son of Man is glorified, and God is glorified in Him. 31 If

God is glorified in Him, God will also glorify Him in Himself, and glorify Him immediately."

He was speaking of His death as a way in which He was glorified, and by which He brought great glory to the Father. To paraphrase verse 32: Since God is glorified by Christ's work on the Cross, God will glorify Him, that is, by raising Him from the dead, and will do it promptly. This is exactly what happened. He raised Him on the third day.

Here are additional verses which speak of the glory of His resurrection and ascension:

Ought not the Christ to have suffered these things and to enter into His glory? (Lk. 24:26)

But this He spoke concerning the Spirit, whom those believing in Him would receive; for the Holy Spirit was not yet given, because Jesus was not yet glorified (Jn. 7:39).

His disciples did not understand these things at first; but when Jesus was glorified, then they remembered that these things were written about Him and that they had done these things to Him (Jn. 12:16).

The God of Abraham, Isaac, and Jacob, the God of our fathers, glorified His Servant Jesus, whom you delivered up and denied in the presence of Pilate, when he was determined to let Him go (Acts 3:13).

...[He was] *received up in glory* (1 Tim. 3:16).

Who through Him [the Lord Jesus] *believe in God, who raised Him from the dead and gave Him glory...* (1 Pet. 1:21).

179

The glory of His resurrection and ascension merges into His eternal glory in heaven. They are inseparable.

The Glory of His Second Coming and Kingdom

There are more references in the New Testament to this glory than to any other. The Son of Man will come in the clouds of heaven with power and great glory (Mt. 24:30). In that day, He will be glorified in His saints and admired among all those who believe (2 Thess. 1:10). When He sits on His glorious throne, He will reward the apostles—and all His followers—(Mt. 19:28), and judge the nations (Mt. 25:31-33). He will be ashamed of those who were ashamed of Him and of His words when He comes in His own glory (Lk. 9:26). James and John unwisely asked to sit to the immediate right and left of Christ in the glory of His coming kingdom (Mk. 10:37). Those who partake of Christ's sufferings now will rejoice with exceeding joy when His glory is revealed in the Millennium (1 Pet. 4:13).

The transfiguration of Christ gave a preview of the Messiah in His glory as King of kings and Lord of lords. Peter, James, and John saw His glory on the holy mountain.

We beheld His glory, the glory as of the only begotten of the Father, full of grace and truth (Jn. 1:14b).

But Peter and those who were with him...when they were fully awake, they saw His glory and the two men who stood with Him (Lk. 9:32).

Peter later referred to the transfiguration and explained that it concerned the power and coming, that is, the coming in power of our Lord Jesus Christ (2 Pet. 1:16).

One other mention of the glory of Christ in His kingdom is

found in John 17:22. There our Great High Priest says:

And the glory which You gave Me I have given them, that they may be one just as We are one.

In one sense, we share some of His glories now—as sons of God, as His brethren, as members of His body, and as joint-heirs with Him.

But in this passage, He is also speaking of His reign on earth as if it were already present. We will share His glory when we reign with Him for one thousand years (Rev. 20:4c). When He is manifested in glory, we will be seen in glory as well.

At the present time, the world neither recognizes nor appreciates God's people.

...Therefore the world does not know us, because it did not know Him (1 Jn. 3:1b).

But when He is manifested in glory, believers will be seen in glory as well:

When Christ who is our life appears, then you also will appear with Him in glory (Col. 3:4).

Beloved, now we are children of God; and it has not yet been revealed what we shall be, but we know that when He is revealed, we shall be like Him, for we shall see Him as He is (1 Jn. 3:2).

Then the world will see the oneness between the Lord Jesus and His followers, will know that the Father sent the Son, and that God loves the saints as He loves His Son.

His Present Glory in Heaven

The desire of the Lord Jesus, as expressed in John 17:24, is that those who love Him might be with Him in heaven, so that they can behold His glory. By faith we can already see Him there, crowned with glory and honor:

But we see Jesus, who was made a little lower than the angels, for the suffering of death crowned with glory and honor, that He, by the grace of God, might taste death for everyone (Heb. 2:9).

His present glory in heaven is the same as what Peter calls His eternal glory:

But may the God of all grace, who called us to His eternal glory by Christ Jesus, after you have suffered a while, perfect, establish, strengthen, and settle you (1 Pet. 5:10).

However, there is one sense in which it is different from His personal glory before He came to earth. He is now in heaven as a *glorified Man* in addition to the glory of His deity.

His present glory is a combination of all His glories, inherent and acquired. It is the glory of His deity, His humanity, His attributes, His offices, and His character. We are not called to share them, but to rejoice in them and to praise Him for them forever.

Endnotes

1 In his beloved Christmas carol, "Hark the Herald Angels Sing."

2 This, incidentally, answers the question, "Could Jesus sin?" He could do only what He saw His Father doing, and this excludes sinning. He always did those things that pleased the Father (Jn. 8:29), and this also excludes sin.

3 This verse could also refer to His moral glory as a Man on earth, but the primary reference is to His transfiguration.

27
Differences in the Gospels

Anyone who studies the Gospels notices that there seems to be a great deal of repetition, especially in Matthew, Mark, and Luke. You read the same miracles, the same parables, and the same messages from the Lord. However, there is no needless repetition. The Holy Spirit never repeats Himself without a reason.

Closer study reveals that it is not the similarities that are important, but the differences. What seem to be repetitions often have slight changes that are highly significant.

Many books have been written listing the harmonies in the Gospels. But they miss the point. It is not the harmonies that matter but the different truths that are brought out in what seem to be the same passages. Let us demonstrate this by comparing similar passages.

In all four Gospels, John the Baptist told his hearers that the Lord would baptize them. When speaking only to believers he said, "He (Jesus) will baptize you with the Holy Spirit" (Mk. 1:8, Jn. 1:33). But when there were unbelievers in his audience, he said, "He will baptize you with the Holy Spirit and with fire" (Mt. 3:11; Lk. 3:16). He was speaking of two different baptisms. The first is a baptism of blessing, the second of judgment.

Two Sermons, Not One

The Sermon on the Mount is found in Matthew 5–7. Parts of it seem to be repeated in Luke 6:17ff. But they are two different messages given on two different occasions. In Matthew the message is delivered on a mountain. In Luke it is a sermon on a plain. Jesus had come down with the disciples and stood on a level place (Lk. 6:17). Matthew describes the ideal citizen of the kingdom, whereas Luke pictures the lifestyle of the disciples as they go forth with the gospel. In Matthew a blessing is pronounced on the poor in spirit (5:3); in Luke the Lord blesses the poor (6:20). There are no woes in Matthew; there are four woes in Luke (6:4-26). These differences should not be passed over quickly and thoughtlessly.

Both Matthew and Luke quote the statement, "The lamp of the body is the eye." In Matthew the context says that the love of money hinders spiritual perception (6:22). In Luke there is no mention of money in the passage (11:33-36). The thought there is that blessing comes through being receptive to the teachings of Jesus and sharing them with others.

Three times in the Gospels, we find the expression, "…with the measure you use, it will be measured back to you." In Matthew 7:2, it is a warning against a judgmental attitude toward others. Mark quotes it as an encouragement to appropriate the Word of God to ourselves (4:24). And Luke uses it to encourage liberality among God's people (6:38).

In Matthew 10:24, Jesus said, "A disciple is not above his teacher, nor a servant above his master." Then in Luke 6:40, He said, "A disciple is not above his teacher, but everyone who is perfectly trained will be as his teacher." They seem to say the same thing, but they are quite different. In Matthew, the Savior is teaching that a disciple cannot expect to be more free from

184

persecution than his Master, whereas in Luke the thought is that a believer cannot lead a disciple beyond the spiritual level that he himself has attained.

The Ninety and Nine

The story of the ninety-nine sheep is a familiar one. In Matthew 18:12-13, it pictures the Lord's love for little children (see v. 14). In Luke 15:4-7 it is aimed at the Pharisees and scribes who were unwilling to acknowledge their need to repent (see vv. 2 and 7).

The parable of the talents (Mt. 25:14-30) must not be confused with the one about the pounds (Lk. 19:12-27). In the case of the talents, three men were given varying amounts of money according to their abilities. The first two received the same commendation in spite of their differing abilities because they were faithful. The third was condemned for failing to do anything with what he had.

In the parable of the pounds, three men received the same amount of money. They all had the same opportunity. One multiplied the money tenfold, another fivefold, and the third not at all. Rewards of the first two differed according to their faithfulness in making the most of what they were given. The third lost what had been given to him.

How Many Denials?

It is possible that Peter denied the Lord at least six times. If we study the Gospels minutely, we find that he denied Christ before: (1) a young woman (Mt. 26:69-70; Mk. 14:66-68); (2) another young woman (Mt. 26:71-72; Mk. 14:69-70); (3) The crowd that stood by (Mt. 26:73-74; Mk. 14:70-71); (4) a man (Lk. 22:58); (5) another man (Lk. 22:59-60); (6) a servant of the high priest (Jn. 18:26-27). This last man is different from the others because he said, "Did I not see you in the garden with Him?" The others are not quoted as saying this.

At the end of each Gospel, the Lord Jesus commissioned His disciples, but notice the different emphasis each time.

Matthew—make disciples, preaching and teaching (28:19)
Mark—preach the gospel (16:15)
Luke—witness (24:48)
John—follow Me (21:19-22)[1]

It is apparent, then, that passages in the Gospels that seem to be the same are not repetition at all. If we carefully examine the differences instead of looking for harmonies, we will find deep spiritual truth. It will solve some seeming contradictions. And it will give us a new appreciation of the marvels of the inspired Word.

Endnote

1 This was spoken to Peter, but it applies to all believers.

SCRIPTURE INDEX

Printed in the United States
41598LVS00001B/1-90